PEOPLE OVER POLITICS

PEOPLE OVER POLITICS

A Nonpartisan Analysis of the Issues
that Matter Most

Antony E. Ghee

Books may be purchased in bulk quantity and/or special sales by contacting the publisher.

Published by Mynd Matters Publishing
715 Peachtree Street NE
Suites 100 & 200
Atlanta, GA 30308
www.myndmatterspublishing.com

e-ISBN: 978-1-957092-43-0 (ebook)
ISBN: 978-1-957092-41-6 (pbk)
ISBN: 978-1-957092-42-3 (hdcv)

FIRST EDITION

In loving memory of my grandfather, Sharpie Ghee, and great-grandparents, Freddie and Catherine Crowder.

To Michele, Taylor, and Jordan for continuing to provide me with my purpose, inspiration, and motivation!

To my mother (Phyllis) and grandmother (Rosa), for providing me with a strong foundation upon which to live my life and consistently encouraging me to pursue my dreams, often in the face of seemingly insurmountable odds!

CONTENTS

INTRODUCTION

"The dogmas of the quiet past are inadequate to the stormy present. The occasion is piled high with difficulty, and we must rise – with the occasion. As our case is new, so we must think anew, and act anew. We must disentrall ourselves, and then we shall save our country."
—Abraham Lincoln

The 2016 election serves as something of a Rubicon in the political history of the United States. What came before seems like another time, even for those of us old enough to remember many of the elections that preceded it. For younger people, in particular, it can seem like their opinions of the political process begin and end with 2016.

In the lead-up to that pivotal election, there was a great deal of debate amongst pundits over why people vote the way they do and whether or not their voting habits align with their interests. Jonathan Haidt, author and professor of psychology at New York University's Stern School of Business, took a different perspective. He said, "Politics at the national level is more like religion than it is like shopping. It's more about a moral vision that unifies a nation and calls it to greatness than it is about self-interest or specific policies."[i]

I wish I could disagree with him.

The idea that a political party should be worshipped like a religion has only grown more common in the last two decades and, since 2016, more fervent. After all, few religions will openly express that *all* members of literally every other religion are evil or, at the very least, immoral. But you find no such compunction when it comes to members of a political party referring to members of other political parties. False narratives encourage people to believe that all Republicans are racist and singularly focused on maximizing their personal wealth at all costs. In response, competing agendas would have you believe that all Democrats are socialists, unpatriotic, and want to destroy the American way of life. Such narratives and broad-based generalizations are not only false, but destructive. Predictably, the rhetoric far too often leads to Americans voting for political candidates who are on their "team" rather than those who actually have a platform that will benefit their interests.

Even worse, it far too often divides families and causes long-standing friendships and relationships to deteriorate. That's the problem with political dogmatism. Emotion replaces rational thought, and inevitably we forget that political parties don't care—people do!

The choice of political party affiliation has become an extremely sensitive issue in social circles. A 2018 Axios poll asked around three thousand adults to select words they would use to describe members of the opposing political party. Survey participants were not asked about specific persons, but rather their overall opinion about every member of the opposing party. I doubt you'll be shocked by the results. Fifty-four percent of Democrats and 49% of Republicans described the opposing party's members as "ignorant." An additional 44% of Democrats and 54% of Republicans described the opposing party's members as "spiteful."

But what about positive attributes? What about descriptors such as "kind," "thoughtful," or "fair?" I won't bore you with the full list, but the highest percentage on either side for any of those words…was just 4%.[ii] In these divided, tribal, and toxic times, it shouldn't be surprising that most Americans are voting for their *team*, rather than their interest.

It seems that many people affiliate with political parties based on the loyalties of their family members and friends and not necessarily based on a thoughtful values-based assessment. Interestingly, some people remain loyal because they fear they will be ostracized from their social circles. So, even as the parties—and the world itself—changes, many people will continue to vote the party line. No doubt, this way of thinking has contributed to rising tensions in modern-day political discourse.

If you're concerned that the purpose of this book is to convince you to change your party affiliation, don't be. Quite the contrary. My goal is to highlight the destructive nature of political polarization and emphasize that no single political party represents the totality of your specific goals and ideals, or the vision you may have for your life and our country. You will realize that it is in your interest to vote based on each candidate's platform, rather than the parenthetical letter—"R" or "D"—next to their name. Ideally, you'll also take a moment to reassess any broad-based assumptions you make about others based solely on how they choose to vote. Ultimately, it will be up to you to assess the topics discussed in this book and decide for yourself where you stand based on your values, experiences, and goals.

I wrote this book for all Americans who despise today's hateful rhetoric and quarreling and don't wish to be stigmatized by their party affiliation or simply because they chose to support a particular candidate. If our nation is to thrive and regain its standing on the world stage, we must be united, notwithstanding inevitable disagreements over policies and tactics.

In certain instances throughout this book, I place special emphasis on African Americans, who are far too often overlooked or taken for granted in the election process. The diversity that exists within the Black community is often ignored, with political strategists from both parties seemingly deciding in advance that they either have the "Black

Vote" locked up or they don't stand a chance at securing a critical mass of support from Black voters. As such, many of the topics covered in this book will accentuate the impact on African Americans.

A Word on Words

Yehuda Berg once said, "Words have energy and power with the ability to help, to heal, to hinder, to hurt, to harm, to humiliate, and to humble." I agree. In fact, I am convinced that part of the problem with our soured discourse—perhaps the largest problem in my opinion—is that words are misused or redefined by candidates and the media for politically-motivated reasons. The lack of consistency in how we define and use words can, in itself, create conflict. Thus, to avoid any confusion, I will define a few popular terms that are often ascribed to people based on their political leanings. All definitions referenced below are derived from traditional sources such as the Merriam-Webster dictionary. I acknowledge, however, that authors of other publications or the creators of social media platforms you follow may use them differently.

Conservative/Right-Winger: Conservatives are often affiliated with the Republican party and are inclined to preserve existing conditions and institutions, have an affinity for tradition, and believe hierarchy is a natural and preferable state of being.

Nationalist: Nationalists strongly identify with their own nation and vigorously support its interests, especially to the exclusion or detriment of other nations. The idea of American Exceptionalism—that the U.S. is inherently different than other nations—is often held by Nationalists. *Please note a Nationalist is NOT the same as a "White Nationalist," which is a term for militant white supremacists who promote and advocate for enforced racial segregation.*

Liberal/Left-Winger: Liberals or left-of-center philosophy generally promotes individual rights, civil liberties, democracy, and freedom from intrusion in private lives. Liberals have traditionally been affiliated with the Democrat party. However, self-identified liberals have become more prevalent in the Republican party since 2016.

Leftist/Progressive: Progressives are generally associated with the Democrat party but are not necessarily liberal. Progressives generally espouse left-wing philosophies that involve implementing social reform, social justice, and top-down policymaking to enforce an equal outcome among disparate groups.

Democratic Socialist: Democratic socialists support political democracy (free and fair elections) but a socially-owned economy. They argue that capitalism is ultimately incompatible with freedom and believe the government should provide essential services (e.g., healthcare) to the public for free, or at a significant discount.

Socialist: Socialists share many beliefs with Democratic Socialists, but they do not believe in free and fair elections. Within a socialist system, the means of production are owned and controlled by the state. American freedoms such as freedom of speech are not compatible with this philosophy.

Communist: Communism adheres to a totalitarian system of government in which a single authoritarian party controls state-owned means of production and there is no right to private property. This is the final stage of society in Marxist theory in which class distinctions cease to exist, and economic goods are distributed equitably according to the state's perception of individual need.

Anarchist: One who believes in a society of complete freedom for individuals without government or any established order.

A Final Thought

Regardless of your race, ethnicity, or sex, it is likely that your views on substantive issues of policy are split between the parties. For example, on the role of the Supreme Court, you may find that your views are fully aligned with the traditional Republican principles, while on matters of our nation's defense, you may find the Democrat party better reflects your expectations of America's role in the world. In either case, you will find no disapproval from me if that should be the case. You are uniquely American and entitled to your own views, values, and beliefs.

My sincerest desire is that the content found within these pages helps you gain a better understanding of the issues impacting our country. Then, when you cast your ballots every two to four years, you will look beyond the red or the blue, the elephant or the donkey, and vote for the candidate whose plan and platform most closely aligns with your values. Understand that no single party holds a patent for good ideas. Progress for our country, and in our respective communities, requires that we evolve beyond a politically polarized existence and find the common ground that strengthens our foundation. It is time that we put people over politics!

CHAPTER 1

THE FUNDAMENTALS OF OUR FOUNDING

★★★★★

"You will never know how much it has cost my generation to preserve your freedom. I hope you will make good use of it."
—John Adams

To understand why the United States government is structured the way it is, you must first understand the world in which it was created. Democratic republics are quite common in the world today, and many nations have enviable legal systems that, like ours, are designed to protect the rights of its citizens. In that context, it can be easy to take for granted—or even forget—that the United States Constitution and its subsequent Bill of Rights were revolutionary in the late 1700s.

Arising from English Common Law

The United States was originally a set of thirteen colonies of the British crown, meaning that its founding fathers were British citizens by birth. They were well-versed in the British legal tradition, which was based on the Magna Carta, written way back in 1215—some 561 years before the United States was founded. The Magna Carta was the first document that we are aware of to state that all people had rights, whether king or pauper. However, the application of that law left something to be desired in the eyes of George Washington, Benjamin Franklin, and the other founders of the United States.

The British Empire was (and is now in its present-day form of the United Kingdom) a Constitutional Monarchy, though at the time, the sovereign had considerably more power than it holds today. England was a Christian country, and its king was believed to be chosen by the Abrahamic God. Thus, to go against the king meant going against God. Under those circumstances, it is easy to see why many people believed the English Common Law didn't quite protect the rights of the common man as much as it was supposed to. The king had supreme authority!

The idea that rights are given to people by their creator, not by the government, as stated in the Constitution, was not only a revolutionary idea, but a treasonous and potentially blasphemous one. The framers wanted to make it clear that no king, no parliament, had the right or authority to deprive a person of their life, liberty, or to obstruct their ability to live their life as they chose (barring due process in the criminal justice system, of course). In English Common Law, you lived and died at the pleasure of the king. Likewise, you prospered at his pleasure. So, if you fell out of the king's favor…you were lucky if you only lost your home, your land, and all your possessions.

However, the delegates to the Constitutional Convention in 1787, though mostly Christian, did not solely use Judeo-Christian traditions and beliefs in crafting the United States Constitution. The central principles undergirding our Constitution—negative rights, delegated powers, checks and balances, and federalism—were also influenced by the ideas of philosophers from the European Enlightenment period, which emphasized notions of liberty, individualism, and separation of church and state, amongst other ideals.

A primary influence was British philosopher John Locke and his ideas on natural rights. The founders, like Locke, believed these natural rights, and the protection thereof, were the whole reason governments should exist. This means the founders believed it is the government's role to protect these natural rights—life, liberty, and property. As Locke himself stated: "Because we are all equal and independent, no-one ought to harm anyone else in his life, health, liberty, or possessions."[iii]

Locke and others of his time also influenced the idea of negative rights, meaning you have the right to be free from attack, the right to be left alone, essentially. This is in contrast to positive rights, which are rights to funds, goods, or services provided by others. Locke and other philosophers of the Enlightenment period also inspired the idea of the separation of powers and checks and balances. Based on these ideas, and in a radical departure from any government structures that existed at the time, the founders decreed a separation of and independence between executive, legislative, and judicial branches to avoid the eventuality of one branch ruling over all others.

Built for Gridlock

Founder James Madison went into great detail regarding the inspiration for and the implementation of the separation of powers, going so far as to emphasize that slow, hindered deliberations—what we commonly call "gridlock"—were ideal for preserving liberty and independence in the long term. He explained the rationale behind the intentional gridlock in Federalist No. 51:

> It may be a reflection on human nature, that such devices [checks and balances] should be necessary to control the abuses of government. But what is government itself, but the greatest of all reflections on human nature? If men were angels, no government would be necessary ... In framing a government which is to be administered by men over men, the great difficulty lies in this: you must first enable the government to control the governed; and in the next place oblige it to control itself. A dependence on the people is, no doubt, the primary control on the government; but experience has taught mankind the necessity of auxiliary precautions.[iv]

Today, many Americans get frustrated with the lengthy process to enact laws, or even pass budgets, wondering, "why can't they just pass it?" The irritation becomes especially palpable when one party controls both chambers of Congress. Why then, should it take so long and be so difficult to pass legislation? Because our system was intentionally designed to be that way.

It is a common misconception that the government formed by our founders is a pure democracy. Not exactly. Our government is best described as a representative republic, one built expressly to prevent, as Madison put it, the "tyranny of the majority." By allowing each of the branches of government the ability to thwart the others, it means for any law to pass (and not be repealed), there has to be broad acceptance of it. That's also why there are two senators from every state, even though different states vary wildly in size and population. Indeed, one could argue that the two-senator rule, in theory, gives too much power to less populated states. But, that's just the point. The founders wanted to ensure the majority could not arbitrarily usurp our government systems and impose its will to subvert the rights of the minority.

Like the Constitution, the Bill of Rights was a novel idea at the time of its creation. The first ten amendments to the Constitution laid out individual rights in a way that no other government had done before. You are likely well aware of some of the amendments in the Bill of Rights, but you may not know them all.

The First Amendment is by far the most often cited, and for good reason. It specifically forbids government encroachment on our speech, our choice of and practice of religion, to assemble and protest (peaceably), and to petition the government to address our grievances. You have likely heard someone say, "I can say whatever I want to!" The First Amendment is what gives them the right to say it.

Even today, our forbearers in the United Kingdom have no right to free speech. And unlike the United States, they have an official religion, even as a declining number of their citizens practice it. Other countries that are, on the surface, very similar to the United States (e.g., Australia), have no right to peaceably assemble. It's easy to forget how rare our freedoms are, even now.

The Second Amendment, which we'll discuss in greater depth in a later chapter, guarantees the right of the people to keep and bear arms. Firearm ownership among the citizenry is legal in many countries, with a variety of restrictions and use cases. Some countries permit only long guns for hunting, while some also allow handguns. Though these nations currently allow their citizens to own weapons, there is nothing stopping their respective governing bodies from taking that right away. Conversely, the U.S. stands as one of three countries in the world with a Constitutional right to own firearms, the others being Mexico and Guatemala.

The Third Amendment protects you from having a soldier quartered in your house without your consent during times of peace. It's hardly a pressing concern in modern times, but it's good to have the assurance anyway.

The Fourth Amendment, like any Law & Order fan knows, protects you from an unreasonable search of your residence or property or confiscation thereof. This amendment is why probable cause must be presented to a judge to secure a warrant prior to a search. By contrast, in England at the time of the Revolution, being a Magistrate or Crown official was sufficient justification to enter someone's home on any random suspicion and take whatever was desired.

The Fifth Amendment protects you from being tried for the same crime twice (double jeopardy) or being compelled to testify against yourself, and it enshrines the requirement for due process. In essence, it protects the public from government persecution and repeatedly being tried for the same crime until the court finds the accused guilty.

The Sixth Amendment ensures the right to a speedy and public trial, by an impartial jury of your peers, to be informed of the charges against you, to confront witnesses against you, and to assist in your own defense.

The establishment of rights articulated in the Fourth and Fifth Amendments were a direct rebuke to the English history of harassing and persecuting anyone they decided were enemies, regardless of whether the person actually broke the law.

The Seventh Amendment ensures a trial by jury in common law, which we now call civil law. Most civil cases are resolved in arbitration and never make it to trial, but it's good to have assurances that you can seek redress from a jury of your peers.

The Eighth Amendment prohibits excessive bail, excessive fines, and cruel and unusual punishments. A simple tour of the Tower of London will give you an idea of what kinds of punishments awaited the Founding Fathers if they were to be captured for treason. England was not alone in its barbarous treatment of prisoners, especially those being interrogated for acts of treason. But the newly minted United States was alone (at the time) in its enshrined prohibition of such acts.

The Ninth Amendment states that if a specific right isn't listed in the Constitution, that does not mean that right should be denied to people.

Finally, the Tenth Amendment mandates that all powers not expressly delegated to the federal government belong to the states or to the people.

These last two amendments, though rarely remembered by the common public, are vitally important. Together, they place a hard limit on the power of the federal government, but no limit on the rights citizens may decide to bestow on themselves through the legislative process. This puts the power in the hands of the people, not a ruling class.

A Divided Perception

My description of the nation's founding has thus far been straightforward. But if you've consumed any media at all in the last ten years, you know that opinions differ vastly regarding our Founding Fathers, the American Revolution, and even the Constitution.

Like most of our modern conflicts, the issue of our founding is split between the political Left and the political Right. The very vocal minorities on the fringes of each political party have staked out opposing, mutually-exclusive positions, with most average American voters not quite sure which side they should be on, or why they are being asked to choose at all.

The Left's View of the Founding

Perhaps the best encapsulation of the far left take on America's founding and its foundational documents can be found in the 1619 Project,[v] a New York Times project directed by Nicole Hannah Jones. A quote from Jones is featured prominently on the project's page: "Our democracy's founding ideals were false when they were written. Black Americans have fought to make them true."

The 1619 Project gives a scholarly voice to the long-held idea that America's entire history was built on the back of slavery and genocide and thus its institutions and traditions should not be upheld. African American and Native American activists have often joined in protests, in legal action, and in lobbying lawmakers to fundamentally change our nation's laws and institutions.

Several of the Founding Fathers, including our first president, George Washington, were slaveholders themselves. This fact, in the eyes of some, discredits their ideas about what a country should be and how it should operate. The disgust with the Founding Fathers has gotten to such a state that statues have been vandalized and toppled.[vi] A statue of Thomas Jefferson, the author of the Declaration of

Independence, was officially removed in New York as a rebuke to his involvement in the slave trade.[vii] In addition to being a slaveholder, Jefferson is known to have fathered several children by one of his slaves, Sally Hemmings.

In both official and unofficial capacities, voices from the Left have risen up to state that the founding was flawed, the men who founded it were flawed, and the country, however well-meaning its current citizens, are simply perpetuating those same flaws. In the most extreme cases, some would argue that we should tear up the Constitution and start over.

Yet, you would be mistaken to assume that this view is attributable only to some black-clad anarcho-communists portrayed on television. Far from it. Many well-respected voices in the modern Democrat party and in academia have espoused similar views. For example, Georgetown law professor Mike Seidman wrote in the New York Times:

> The people who wrote the Constitution lived in a small rural country, huddled along the Eastern Seaboard — a large part of which was financed by slave labor. ...Many of them believed that it was okay to own other human beings. Almost all of them believed that women should have no role in public affairs. Almost all of them believed people...without property have no role in public affairs. Why on earth would anybody think that their decisions ought to bind us now?[viii]

On local, state, and federal levels, people and organizations that share these beliefs advocate to pass new laws and change existing ones with a view towards re-imagining and re-shaping the country. In their view, the foundation upon which our country was built can never produce a righteous legal or legislative system.

The Right's View of the Founding

Far from their counterpart's assertion that the founding was inherently flawed, the activists and personalities on the Right often argue that the founding documents are the only sources of legitimate authority in the United States. In the recent appointment of Supreme Court Justice Amy Coney Barrett, part of what made her so appealing to the Right was her being an "originalist," meaning that in her interpretations of law, she focuses on the constitutional text and what the framers had in mind when the Constitution was ratified. This, to those on the Right, is exceptionally appealing because they hold the creation of the United States to be special, perhaps even sacred.

Politically engaged Christian pastors such as Billy Graham and later, Jerry Falwell, have often made the claim that the U.S. is under God's protection, that God was present at the founding, and the U.S. is unequivocally a Christian nation. Not all people on the Right are aligned with the Evangelical movement, but most view the founding documents and the government formed by the Founding Fathers to be the best possible form of government in the world. The Right very much aligns with Ronald Regan's designation of the U.S. as a "shining city on a hill."

In contrast to the Left, the Right does not believe the stain of slavery on the history of America is the country's defining characteristic. They also reject the notion that the U.S. is uniquely evil for having had slaves at its founding, pointing to the Barbary slave trade in North Africa and the fact that slavery was only outlawed in Saudi Arabia in 1960. In fact, many people will be shocked to learn that slavery still exists in some countries today.

Daily Wire founder Ben Shapiro notes that America was founded in spite of slavery, not because of it. And though the U.S. was not unique in having slaves for part of its history, it was unique for abolishing it, taking the extra step of losing thousands of lives in a Civil

War to finally be rid of it.[ix]

When groups and individuals on the Right lobby their legislators and public officials for changes in the law or in policy, they do so with the firm intent of going back to what the Founders intended, rather than asking for an entirely new way of doing things. The problems we are having, they argue, arise because we have gotten away from our roots. If we return to the way things were meant to be, these problems would not exist.

Determining the Way Forward

Most Americans can look at views from the Left and Right and find flaws in both. In fact, 80% of Americans believe the answers lie somewhere in the middle. Of course, some changes may be prudent to accommodate a modern society but let's not destroy the entire foundation of the democracy. The more sensible approach, in my humble opinion, is to elect leaders who will unite the masses around fundamentally sound principles of governing and implement responsible reforms to the existing system. But, therein lies the challenge. The "system" is so complex and broad that it can encompass many aspects of our government and country. Therefore, we must be specific with our requests when pressing our elected officials to take action.

Ask yourself what you think is "broken" in our country. It may be helpful to first consider issues in your own community or state. For example, does your community have a failing public school system, inadequate medical care, insufficient childcare resources, an unacceptable rate of unemployment or high rates of crime? Do you believe those problems stem from a single point of failure or are they attributable to broader societal issues? How do you want your elected officials to resolve these problems? If the candidate is an incumbent, has their voting history and tactics improved your life or produced meaningful positive changes within your community? If not, why should you continue to vote for him or her? In any event, you are likely to be much more effective in your effort to press for change if you raise specific concerns rather than making vague or general demands to your elected officials to fix the "system."

Within our government, there are many roles with differing degrees of influence. The great news is our country's founding fathers established a framework that allows us to decide who fills those roles, and ultimately helps to fix whatever we believe is broken. It's true your preferred candidate may not always win, but your voice and your vote counts. Whether you wish to somehow improve the "system" that currently exists or tear it down and replace it with a new one, determining whether a candidate aligns with your values and beliefs is a vital first step.

In some countries, you will have several candidates to choose from in each election, and there may be a panoply of political parties to serve a variety of interests. But in the United States, for all intents and purposes, there are only two political parties that garner most of the attention and resources. These two parties—Democrats and Republicans—are what you will most consistently find on the ballot when you cast your vote every two to four years. Let's talk about what that means for you.

CHAPTER 2
POLITICAL PARTIES
★★★★★

"I was no party man myself, and the first wish of my heart was if parties did exist, to reconcile them."

—George Washington

"In truth, I care little about any party's politics...the man behind it is the important thing."

—Mark Twain

The **Democrats** and **Republicans** are the two main political parties that the average voter is asked to choose between. There are, of course, other parties such as the Libertarian party and the Green party. There are also registered Independents. However, officeholders at the federal level are nearly always from the two major parties and, on the rare occasion a third-party candidate makes an appearance in a national contest, it is even more unusual for them to win. For that reason, this chapter will focus on the two major parties in American politics.

History the Modern Parties

Some of the Founding Fathers, George Washington in particular, distrusted political parties and advised against dividing the electorate into factions. However, Thomas Jefferson held a different perspective, stating, "Men by their constitutions are naturally divided into two parties."[x] Looking at the history of our political parties, it's difficult to disagree with him.

The Republicans – The Party and its Presidents

The Republican Party, often called the GOP (short for "Grand Old Party") was founded in 1854 specifically to combat slavery from being instituted in the western territories. Very often, the GOP is referred to as "The party of Lincoln," because of its slavery-fighting roots and for the party affiliation of our sixteenth president.

The Kansas-Nebraska Act of 1854 would have permitted slavery in new U.S. territories by popular referendum. The legislation prompted widespread anger from members of the now-defunct Whig party as well as dissatisfied Democrats. Together, they founded the new Republican Party with the goal of preventing the expansion of slavery westward, rather than its outright abolition. To be clear, the Republican goal was not to abolish slavery in the South right away. Rather, they sought to prevent its expansion westward because they feared that slaveholding interests would dominate national politics. Ultimately, slavery and debates about territories in which slavery should exist were the pivotal issues that sparked the Civil War in 1861.

Abraham Lincoln, a Republican, won the presidency in 1860 and ultimately presided over the Civil War. He issued the Emancipation Proclamation in 1863 and oversaw the passage of the Thirteenth Amendment, which abolished slavery.

It was during Reconstruction, in the aftermath of the Civil War, that Republicans first became associated with big business. During that time, they worked to expand economic activity in the country by increasing the federal government's spending in conjunction with Northern financiers and industrialists.

By the time of the Great Depression, Republicans were viewed as the party of the wealthy, with little to offer working-class people. They were largely blamed for the stock market crash of 1929 and criticized for a perceived lack of government intervention to help the people suffering during the Depression. Incumbent President Herbert Hoover was most especially reviled.

He served one term in office from 1929-1933 and it would be another twenty years before another Republican was elected president. That honor would be bestowed upon President Dwight Eisenhower, a well-regarded Army General and World War II veteran. Eisenhower was a popular president and served two terms in office from 1953-1961. During Eisenhower's tenure, the U.S. experienced unprecedented economic growth and solidified its presence as a world power. A little-known fact–President Eisenhower also signed into law the Civil Rights Act of 1957, which was the first federal civil rights legislation and oversaw the creation of the U.S. Commission on Civil Rights, and the Department of Justice's Civil Rights Division.

Eight years after President Eisenhower's tenure concluded, his vice president, Richard Nixon, assumed the office of the president in 1969. President Nixon's tenure, however, was marred by the Vietnam War and the infamous Watergate scandal, in which key members of his administration were convicted for engaging in illegal activities to sabotage their political opponents. President Nixon was impeached for his involvement in the scandal and resigned from office in 1974.

Following Nixon's resignation, his vice president, Gerald Ford, assumed the office of the president but lost the ensuing election in 1976. His failed election campaign was likely no surprise because many Americans were upset that he pardoned President Nixon for his role in the Watergate scandal and the U.S. was in the midst of a severe economic downturn. To his credit, President Ford officially recognized Black History Month in 1976, calling on Americans to "seize the opportunity honor the too often neglected accomplishments of Black Americans in every area of endeavor throughout our history."

As an aside, the notable historian Carter G. Woodson established Negro History Week in 1926 to amplify Black history and culture. By officially recognizing Black History Month, President Ford amplified the efforts of Carter G. Woodson some fifty years earlier to ensure that African American history was not only preserved but celebrated and enshrined within American history. But I digress...

Following the recession and economic stagnation of the 1970s, Americans wanted a change. In 1980, President Ronald Regan, a former actor, won the presidency by campaigning on a platform that promised to bring prosperity back to Americans through smaller government, tax cuts, and reduced regulations on businesses.

President Reagan's economic policies (often referred to as "Reaganomics") stimulated the economy and he successfully maneuvered the U.S. through a Cold War with the Soviet Union. His popularity soared and he was elected to a second term. However, his Republican successor, George H.W. Bush, proved to be less popular and served only one term before being defeated by Democrat Bill Clinton in the 1992 presidential election. Despite an economically successful eight-year tenure, President Clinton was succeeded by Republican George W. Bush, who narrowly won a controversial election in 2000 that required Supreme Court intervention.

Despite the election controversy, President Bush is credited with appointing the first African American Secretary of State when he appointed the highly-decorated and well-respected retired Army General Colin Powell to the post in 2001. He appointed Powell's successor too—Condoleezza Rice. She was the first female African American to serve as Secretary of State and the first woman to serve on the National Security Council.

In 2008, the U.S. economy plunged into a massive recession. In addition, the U.S. was engulfed in the increasingly unpopular post-9-11 military conflicts in Iraq and Afghanistan. Ultimately, the

Republican party bore much of the blame for both in the media. Republican candidate John McCain lost the ensuing election to Democrat Barack Obama, who captivated the nation with a message of hope on his way to making history, becoming the first African American to be elected president of the United States.

President Obama won reelection in 2012. After his two terms in office, he was succeeded by President Donald Trump, who ran as a Republican. President Trump implemented what he called an "America First" policy, which emphasized nationalism while lowering expectations for America's involvement in international affairs. Most would likely be surprised to learn that the "America First" policy was first coined by President Woodrow Wilson, a Democrat. But, as stated earlier, neither party has a patent on good (or bad) ideas.

President Trump saw value in the tagline and he used it. He implemented his version of the policy and began withdrawing military troops from the twenty-year quagmire in the Middle East and focused on growing the U.S. economy. During President Trump's tenure, the unemployment rate for African Americans reached an all-time low of 5.5%. However, any economic progress he achieved was offset by a period of social unrest and the start of the Coronavirus Pandemic. When all was said and done, President Trump served only one term in office, losing his reelection bid in 2020 to Democratic senator and former vice president, Joe Biden.

Today's GOP is generally described as being more fiscally and socially conservative than Democrats and it favors smaller government, less regulation, lower taxes, and less federal intervention in the economy. In the early 2000s, the Republican party had well-publicized affiliations with the Evangelical Christian movement and, though those ties remain, Republicans are less likely to describe themselves as a Christian party, as its younger members, like Americans in general, often gravitate toward other religions or no religion at all.

The Republican platform, which was most recently updated in 2016, states:

Republicans believe in liberty, economic prosperity, preserving American values and traditions, and restoring the American dream for every citizen of this great nation. As a party, we support policies that seek to achieve those goals.

Our platform is centered on stimulating economic growth for all Americans, protecting constitutionally guaranteed freedoms, ensuring the integrity of our elections, and maintaining our national security. We are working to preserve America's greatness for our children and grandchildren.

The Republican Party's legacy—we were originally founded in 1854 for the purpose of ending slavery —compels us to patriotically defend America's values. As the left attempts to destroy what makes America great, the Republican Party is standing in the breach to defend our nation and way of life.[xi]

As you can see, the modern Republican party fully embraces a Conservative philosophy, one that seeks a secure, profitable, and free existence for Americans. Each party votes on its platform on a regular basis, so it is reasonable to assume that a candidate running on the GOP ticket will abide by these principles. However, as stated earlier, it is important to assess each candidate individually to ensure they have truly embraced these ideals. As Mark Twain stated, "It's not about a party's politics, the man behind it is the important thing."

The Democrats – The Party and its Presidents
The Democratic Party is the nation's oldest existing political party and is now perceived as an advocate for a strong federal government and

supporter of minority rights, workplace and educational equity, environmental protection, and progressive reforms.

The party we now call the Democrats was formed in 1792 by supporters of Thomas Jefferson and James Madison, calling themselves the Democratic-Republicans. The party spawned several presidents throughout the 1800s, including Andrew Jackson and John Quincy Adams. In fact, Democrats would win all but two presidential elections from 1828 to 1856.

Ironically, the Kansa-Nebraska Act, which led to the formation of the Republican party, also resulted in a split among the Democrats, with Southern Democrats favoring slavery in all territories, and Northerners preferring that each territory decide for itself via popular referendum. The disagreement likely contributed to Democrat Stephen Douglas losing to Abraham Lincoln in the 1860 presidential election.

During the Reconstruction era that followed the Civil War, the Democratic Party developed a stronghold in the South and strongly opposed the Reconstruction-allied Republicans support of "big business" interests. The Democrats held firmly to this position and, by the end of the nineteenth century, established their brand as the party of rural workers and conservative values.

However, at the turn of the century, the Democrats experienced yet another division, this time between its conservative and progressive members. After the Democrats lost the presidential election in 1896, the progressive wing of the party solidified itself as the dominant force within the party for the next thirty years. When the Great Depression struck in 1929, the progressives were well positioned to aggressively advance their agenda.

In 1932, Franklin D. Roosevelt became the first Democrat to win the White House since Woodrow Wilson concluded his term as president in 1921. During his first 100 days in office, President

Roosevelt launched a slew of federal programs cumulatively known as the "New Deal." President Roosevelt's tenure marked the beginning of what is often called the Progressive Era.

Despite their years of dominance and control at the federal level during the Progressive Era, Democrats were not unified. The Civil Rights movement and the fight to end racial segregation were wildly unpopular among Southern Democrats, often called Dixiecrats at that time. In 1948, after President Harry Truman (himself a Southern Democrat) introduced a pro-civil rights platform, a group of Southerners walked out of the party's national convention and ran their own candidate for president.

But it was Democratic President Lyndon B. Johnson who signed the Civil Rights Act of 1964 and the Voting Rights Act of 1965 into law, bolstering the protections provided in the Civil Rights Act of 1957 passed during Republican President Dwight Eisenhower's administration. President Johnson is also credited with appointing Thurgood Marshall to the Supreme Court. Justice Marshall was a civil rights icon and the first African American to serve on the Supreme Court, a position he held from 1967 to 1991. These actions contributed to a shift of white Southerners from the Democrat party to the Republican party, a trend that accelerated in the 1960s during the civil rights riots. Around the same time, many African American voters who had staunchly identified with the Republican party since the Civil War started voting for Democrats, a trend that continues to this day.

Democrats lost five out of six presidential elections from 1968 to 1988, but regained the White House in 1992 when Arkansas Governor Bill Clinton defeated the incumbent President George H.W. Bush, a Republican. President Clinton received tremendous support from the African American community. He served two terms in office and his tenure is considered by some to be a golden age of sorts, marked by economic prosperity, technical innovation, and a sense of general optimism among the American public. His presidency, however, had its share of controversies and scandals. President Clinton was impeached by the Republican-majority House in 1998 for allegedly lying under oath to a federal grand jury and obstructing justice. Ultimately, he was acquitted, but the proceedings were viewed by many Americans to be of a partisan nature and were not popular.[xii]

Despite the economic prosperity that accompanied the Clinton presidency, his vice president, Al Gore, narrowly lost the 2000 election to Republican George W. Bush after the U.S. Supreme Court halted a manual recount of disputed Florida ballots.

President Bush's presidency was marred by foreign affairs and international military conflicts, as well as the onset of the Great Recession of 2008. Those issues paved the way for then-Senator Barack Obama of Illinois to ascend to the highest office in the land after his popularity surged when he delivered a powerful message of hope at the Democratic National Convention. His speech galvanized the Democrats and many others across the political spectrum as he proceeded to make history, becoming the first African American president of the United States.

After President Obama served two terms in office, the next Democratic nominee could have made history as the first female president had she won the 2016 election. Former Senator and Secretary of State Hillary Clinton (and wife of former President Bill Clinton) ran on the Democrat ticket, but was defeated by Republican Donald Trump, a political outsider, business mogul, and reality television star. By many accounts, President Trump's election was considered a political upset, but he had a massive following of supporters that carried him to the White House.

In 2020, Hillary Clinton announced she would not run again for the office of the president. President Obama's former vice president, Joe Biden, stepped in to lead the Democratic ticket and defeated the incumbent, President Trump.

Recent history has shown that the party from which presidents are elected is prone to change more frequently than in past decades. That should come as no surprise as the parties themselves are in transition. For example, today's Democrats have cemented their party's progressive message. However, that wasn't always the case. The party's message has evolved and is vastly different from what it was in the 1960s, a fact which Democratic leadership will proudly share.

A major pillar of the Democrat platform is the belief that free markets are unfair and, if left unregulated, dangerous to the prosperity and wellbeing of Americans. They argue that government regulations and programs are necessary to provide assistance to those who need it most. The Democratic Platform, ratified in 2020, is an impressive 92 pages, so I hope you'll forgive me for not including the full text as I did for the Republicans. Their major tenets are as follows:

1. *Building a stronger, fairer economy*
2. *Achieving universal, affordable, quality health care*
3. *Protecting communities and building trust by reforming our criminal justice system*
4. *Healing the soul of America*
5. *Combatting the climate crisis and pursuing environmental justice*
6. *Restoring and strengthening our democracy*
7. *Creating a 21ˢᵗ-century immigration system*
8. *Providing a world-class education in every zip code*
9. *Renewing American leadership*

As younger Democrats get elected or appointed to political positions in the House and Senate, it is likely that the party platform will continue to evolve. But for now, Democrats have allied themselves with a progressive agenda, seeking to displace current practices in search of what they believe is a more equitable society.

The Common Thread

As you read through the progression of presidents over the centuries, you likely noticed that prior to the late 20th century, one party held the presidency for a steady block of time before control reverted to the other party. However, starting in the 1970s, this ceased to be the case. Why? To quote political advisor James Carville, former campaign manager for Bill Clinton in the 1992 election: "It's the economy, stupid!" Culture wars often drive media headlines. However, the media's focus, as well as the interest of the American public, quickly shifts when the economy is in a slump.

It is logical to assume that Americans vote for and elect candidates they believe will improve their lives. Thus, if their business is suffering or they lose their job in a recession, they would be less likely to vote for the candidate or party that was in office when their fortunes declined. However, because the United States is not a pure democracy, the person who wins the presidential election isn't necessarily the person who won the majority of the popular vote. Likewise, the party that wins the presidency and/or control of the House or Senate isn't always the most beloved. When that happens, it is easy to understand why segments of the American population could feel disconnected from their elected officials, especially if they do not believe they are benefiting from the country's general prosperity?

Where are African Americans in Party Politics?

This type of alienation, a sense of being deprived of the American dream, is exactly the feeling that has caused as many as 90% of African Americans to consistently vote Democrat since the 1960s. Prior to the Civil Rights Movement, African Americans consistently voted for the Republican party, and for good reason. The Republicans were the party formed entirely to fight slavery and the first Republican president ended slavery in the United States. Additionally, Southern Democrats were the ones who impeded Reconstruction efforts, promoted sharecropping and supported Jim Crow laws, which were designed to force racial segregation and ensure African Americans remained a subjugated class. Under those circumstances, it was not hard for African Americans to see which party aligned with their interests, and they voted accordingly.

But time passed…and times changed. Enduring prejudice and race-based violence was not confined to those living in the South, and when the stock market crashed in 1929, jobs became scarce. African Americans suffered right along with other Americans and the Republican party, which they had supported for decades, had no help to give them, or anyone else, it seemed. But then came the election of President Franklin D. Roosevelt and the subsequent passage of the New Deal, causing many African Americans to reconsider their political allegiance.

Most African Americans were skeptical about benefiting from the New Deal, and racial discrimination remained rampant. However, a cohort of black advisors and activists critiqued these government programs for excluding African Americans and enacted some reforms. At the grassroots level, black workers pressed for expanded employment opportunities and joined new labor unions to fight for economic rights.[xiii]

During the 20th century, African Americans continued to fight for their freedom and battled for their political voices to be heard. They primarily supported Democrats despite the fact that Democrats were no friendlier to African Americans than Republicans.

Even as President Lyndon B. Johnson maneuvered to pass the Civil Rights Act of 1964, he was seemingly no friend to African Americans, using the "N-word" prolifically in private (and not-so-private) conversations with colleagues. It appears that his motivation for even considering the Civil Rights Act of 1964 had less to do with promoting equality and dignity for African Americans, and more to do with craven political ambition. "I'll have these n***ers voting Democrat for 200 years," he was reported to have said.[xiv]

Unsurprisingly, this crude cynicism inspired a healthy skepticism among African American leaders in both parties. Malcolm X gave his famous "Ballot or the Bullet" speech in 1964, an election year, in which he urged African Americans to look beyond parties and to vote their interests. In Malcolm's view, it was imperative that African Americans look after themselves because white Americans, regardless of party, would not.

I'm not a politician, not even a student of politics; in fact, I'm not a student of much of anything. I'm not a Democrat. I'm not a Republican, and I don't even consider myself an American. If you and I were Americans, there'd be no problem. Those [white people] that just got off the boat, they're already Americans; [the Polish] are already Americans; the Italian refugees are already Americans. Everything that came out of Europe, every blue-eyed thing, is already an American. And as long as you and I have been over here, we aren't Americans yet...

In this present administration, they have in the House of Representatives 257 Democrats to only 177 Republicans. They control two-thirds of the House vote. Why can't they pass something that will help you and me? In the Senate, there are 67 senators who are of the Democratic Party. Only 33 of them are Republicans. Why, the Democrats have got the government sewed up, and you're the one who sewed it up for them. And what have they given you for it? Four years in office, and just now getting around to some civil-rights legislation...I'm not trying to knock out the Democrats for the

Republicans. We'll get to them in a minute. But it is true; you put the Democrats first and the Democrats put you last…

I say again, I'm not anti-Democrat, I'm not anti-Republican, I'm not anti-anything. I'm just questioning their sincerity, and some of the strategy that they've been using on our people by promising them promises that they don't intend to keep. When you keep the Democrats in power, you're keeping the Dixiecrats in power … That's why, in 1964, it's time now for you and me to become more politically mature and realize what the ballot is for; what we're supposed to get when we cast a ballot; and that if we don't cast a ballot, it's going to end up in a situation where we're going to have to cast a bullet. It's either a ballot or a bullet.[xv]

Notably, Malcolm X's famous speech was given in a Christian church, even though he, of course, was an avowed Muslim. The church has historically been the center of African American political life and, even in today's more secular times, the church still holds sway in the African American community. Yet, today's church is evolving like so many other faith-based institutions and aptly trying to determine how it can best serve the community. One author astutely posed the question: "Should it carry forward the prophetic imperative of the civil rights movement, the collective mandate for social change? Or, should it focus on personal prosperity and individual economic advancement?"[xvi]

The author recognizes that the "prosperity gospel is sometimes linked to social conservatism." It is interesting then that since the mid-1960s, a substantial majority of African Americans have consistently voted for one party. However, their views and those of the Black church on substantive policy issues ironically are often divided between the parties, evidenced by a mix of socially-conservative values and fiscally-liberal preferences.

Beyond the Slogans

It is important to understand that parties, in and of themselves, do not and cannot solve any of the problems plaguing our communities. Political parties are comprised of people who may have different values, agendas, and even competing priorities. Therefore, a candidate who only comes to your neighborhood or speaks to your community during election season should be viewed with a healthy dose of skepticism, even if they have your preferred letter—an "R" or "D"—after their name. Even though the political parties serve as a rough guide to a candidate's beliefs and intended course of action, ultimately, each candidate must be judged on their own merits.

Indeed, every two to four years, Americans are asked to choose their local, state, and national representatives. I urge you to be thoughtful in your analysis and make an informed decision about which candidate most closely shares your values and will best advance your interests, economically, socially, or otherwise. It sounds like a straightforward process, but it isn't. In truth, it never has been and never will be because neither party and no single candidate likely represents the totality of your views and beliefs.

CHAPTER 3
VOTING & VOTING RIGHTS

"We do not have a government by the majority. We have a government by the majority who participate."
—Thomas Jefferson

There's a famous scene in Martin Scorsese's film *Gangs of New York*, where Amsterdam, played by Leonardo DiCaprio, lines up Irish immigrants to vote for the Tammany-backed candidate for sheriff. Once each man casts his vote, he's given a shave and a change of clothes and sent back to vote again, resulting in more votes for the sheriff than there were citizens of New York City. Obviously, it's a movie and not necessarily historically accurate, but American elections have always been fraught things. "Does my vote count?" Americans ask themselves. The questions surrounding fairness and accuracy in elections may have improved since the Tammany Hall days, but that doesn't mean they don't exist.

Votes are counted in a variety of ways, depending upon the state and district in which a person is voting. All elections, both at the state and federal level, are run by state governments, which is why there is so much variation in the rules surrounding voting—the machines used to cast votes, and the requirements to be eligible to vote in elections. Computer touch screens, punch cards, and of course, pen-and-paper ballots are used across the country, and the methods of counting and certifying the votes are every bit as variable.

Punch cards are the least frequently used method, as voter confidence in them took a dive in the 2000 presidential election when the Republican candidate George W. Bush defeated the Democratic candidate, Al Gore. Florida used the punch card ballots and an abnormally high number of votes were counted for third-party candidate Pat Buchanan. Even Buchanan himself admitted it was unlikely so many Floridians had voted for him to be president and, in looking at the layout of the punch cards, many people admitted they were confusing. Of course, that was only part of the confusion of that election, but that's not the focus of this book. The broader point is that there are a variety of ways to vote and the method chosen is determined by the state or locale in which you reside.

Whose Vote Should Count?

In the last decade, there have been increasing calls to grant noncitizens the right to vote in elections. These calls for change, led entirely by Democrats, have resulted in legislative enactments in many cities, including the city of New York.

The "Our City, Our Vote" measure that recently passed in New York was designed to grant more than 800,000 noncitizens and "Dreamers" in New York the right to have access to voting in municipal elections as early as next year. To be clear, the bill applies to noncitizens who are in the United States legally, not undocumented residents of New York.

Proponents of the bill—among them, Attorney Raul Reyes—celebrate this law: "Allowing noncitizens to vote in local elections is smart policy that is legally sound. It will strengthen communities and give more residents an investment in politics that affect their daily lives. And allowing noncitizens to vote is rooted in both American tradition and ideals."[xvii]

Opponents, not necessarily all Republicans, have promised to challenge the new law, arguing that even municipal-level elections should not be open to foreign nationals as it constitutes foreign interference in U.S. Elections.

New York is certainly not the only city to permit noncitizens to cast ballots. More than a dozen municipalities across the United States, primarily in Democrat-controlled municipalities located on the coasts, already allow noncitizens to vote in local elections. However, they are not permitted to vote in federal elections for the president or members of Congress, nor are they permitted to vote for the governor, judges, or state legislators.

The question posed by Republicans and other opponents of legislative initiatives granting voting rights to noncitizens is why citizens of other countries should be permitted to influence our elections and policies. And why, in the case of New York's legislation, should noncitizens be given the right vote on municipal-level matters but not state matters? The short answer—it's simply a matter of jurisdiction.

In 1996, Congress prohibited noncitizens from voting in federal elections, but the language in, and interpretation of, state constitutions vary. It is true that no state explicitly authorizes noncitizens to vote in statewide elections (e.g., for governor) and state-level legislation would need to be passed to authorize it. However, vague or ambiguous language in a state's constitution may leave just enough room for local authorities to claim jurisdiction and implement such initiatives on the basis that those elections fall within their purview.

The problem (or benefit, depending on your perspective) is these laws are being passed based on the preferences of the politicians, not the citizens of the city. This means if a citizen of New York doesn't like the idea of noncitizens voting in municipal elections, then he or she cannot vote against the measure itself. Instead, the citizen would most likely have to wait until the next election to vote against the politicians who passed the legislation. Under those circumstances, it may feel like your vote doesn't count for much.

Are Driver's License Requirements Inherently Racist?

Though the New York law and others like it are specifically designed to enfranchise noncitizens who are here legally, there is also a concern that votes may be cast by people who are *not* in this country legally. To ensure that only individuals permitted to vote are the ones actually casting a vote on election day, it has long been a requirement to show photo identification at polling places.

Primarily Democratic activists and politicians advocate for eliminating requirements for photo identification. Their rationale is that photo identification can be onerous for lower-income citizens to acquire, especially those who are elderly and may lack the necessary paperwork to satisfy their state's requirements. But the loudest voices decry requirements for photo identification at polling places as a racist holdover from the Jim Crow era, once designed to disenfranchise Black people.

In September 2021, North Carolina judges seemed to agree with that view when the court struck down the state's voter photo identification law. Two of the three presiding judges concluded that the law was unconstitutional because it intentionally discriminated against Black voters. The law "was motivated at least in part by an unconstitutional intent to target African American voters," Superior Court Judges Michael O'Foghludha and Vince Rozier wrote in the 100-page majority opinion. Furthermore, "Other, less restrictive voter I.D. laws would have sufficed to achieve the legitimate nonracial purposes of implementing the constitutional amendment requiring voter I.D., deterring fraud, or enhancing voter confidence."[xviii]

Of course, the judges were examining a specific law and the specific circumstances under which it was passed. No doubt, some legal scholars will take issue with the court's judicial reasoning but arguments in support of, or in opposition to, are beyond the scope of this book. However, nearly all reasonable minds would likely agree that a finding of racial bias in one law does not mean that all photo identification requirements are inherently racist and designed to keep minorities from voting.

Journalist Ami Horowitz went viral in 2016 with a video in which he interviewed a collection of mostly young, college-aged white people, who all agreed it was racist to ask African Americans to acquire photo identification. When asked to explain their rationale, the young people gave a variety of reasons why it "wasn't okay" to ask African Americans to present photo identification to vote. One person indicated that African Americans did not have cell phones or access to the internet. Another argued that African Americans couldn't possibly afford the fee to get a driver's license. And yet another surmised that African Americans were frequently "convicted felons" and couldn't find their way to the Department of Motor Vehicles (DMV). Wow!

Horowitz then interviewed a range of college-age to middle-age African Americans in Harlem. The interviewees responded to Horowitz's questions, often with a perplexed look on their faces. Why, yes, they did have a driver's license. All of them. More to the point, they didn't know anyone who didn't have one. "How you gonna get on a plane without an I.D.?" asked one of the interviewees.[xix] Likewise, they also knew the location of the nearest DMV, each of them had internet access in their home, and a younger interviewee was quite pleased to pull out his phone.

The experiment was hardly scientific, and it has been a long-running prank to target unassuming young people and film their sometimes-hilarious responses to basic questions. But it did give some perspective to unsettling misperceptions that African Americans are the ones primarily resisting photo identification requirements at polling places. Quite the contrary, African Americans are just as likely to have identification as every other race of Americans. In fact, some are personally offended by the notion that they do not. Under those circumstances, it is not surprising that some would argue that the resistance to photo identification requirements stems not from a concern for African Americans, but more likely for noncitizens who are less likely to have photo identification.

Voting and the Vocal Minority

Most Americans do not vote and, if they do, it is typically during presidential elections. The 2020 presidential election had one of the highest recorded turnouts, with 159 million ballots cast. That represents only 66.7% of the eligible voting population of 239 million Americans. This is a significant increase from 2016, when there were 137.5 million votes cast out of an eligible 224 million American citizens aged 18 or older (~60%).[xx] Having only 60% of eligible voters show up to vote in a hotly-contested presidential election may not seem terribly impressive and, by some other countries' standards, it isn't. But, it is an incredible turnout when you consider how few Americans vote in midterm elections and even fewer in primary elections.

In recent years, it may appear that many of our legislators have drifted farther to the fringes of their respective political parties because, to put it bluntly, they have. This is largely due to a process colloquially called "primarying." Long-serving congresspeople and senators are most likely from districts that typically only vote for one party. For instance, House Speaker Nancy Pelosi represents California's 12th District, which has been a Democratic stronghold that hasn't elected a Republican to the House of Representatives since 1990, and that was an outlier. So, if Speaker Pelosi's constituents became displeased with her service, chances are slim to none that they would vote for a Republican candidate in an attempt to defeat her in the general election.

However, there is the possibility of finding another Democrat, one more in line with what the people of the 12th District want, and have that candidate run against Nancy Pelosi in the Democratic primary. This is only an example, of course. Primary challenges against high-profile incumbents are typically unsuccessful unless they have seriously run afoul of their constituents. Primary challenges most often afflict long-running politicians who don't have a high profile. In some cases, constituents don't even know the representative's name. These are the candidates most vulnerable to a primary challenge launched by a new, unknown, and usually more partisan politician.

A recent example of a successful primary challenge involved Democratic Congresswoman Alexandria Ocasio-Cortez of New York. In 2018, AOC, as she is commonly known, ran a primary challenge against incumbent Congressman Joe Crowley, who had held his seat since 2009. At only twenty-nine years of age, she was the youngest person to ever be elected to Congress and she won without the help of any political action committees (PACs). Like Nancy Pelosi's district in California, AOC's New York district consistently votes for Democratic candidates in general elections. Thus, their primary elections are more important since the results of the general election are never really in question.

Though Joe Crowley was hardly a centrist, his voting record led his constituents to question whether he was liberal enough, whereas AOC was firmly in the progressive camp. In addition to having endorsements from Black Lives Matter and the National Abortion Rights Action League (NARAL)—both popular organizations in her district—AOC is Hispanic, which more closely reflects the demographics of New York's 14th district. Fewer than 30,000 votes were cast in that primary election. So, with a mere 16,898 votes, Alexandria Ocasio-Cortez secured a congressional seat. But don't criticize AOC, this is how our system works.

AOC wasn't the only progressive to unseat a more moderate Democrat and, on the other side of the political aisle, multiple moderate Republicans were unseated in primaries by candidates who held more partisan views. In 2020, two of those moderates were Denver Riggleman of Virginia and Scott Tipton of Colorado. In both instances, the victors in those primary elections held views that were far less moderate than their opponents and both went on to win the general election, thus widening the chasm between the Left and the Right.

The presidential elections are the ones that garner the most attention. They are the ones that captivate us and make us feel like "it's all on the line." And it is. For every person who has ever voted in a presidential election, I salute you. And I hope you vote in the next one too. But I also hope you will come to understand and appreciate the importance of voting in all elections, the ones where you choose your school board members, vote on ballot initiatives for a new community pool, and any other matter that impacts your community and our country. That includes voting in the often overlooked but ever more important primary elections. If you choose to forfeit your right to vote in primary elections, you waive the privilege of influencing which candidates will ultimately represent your party in the general election. As civil rights activist and Congressman John Lewis stated: "The vote is precious. It is almost sacred. It's the most powerful and non-violent tool we have in a democratic society, and we've got to use it."

By now, it should be clear that it is not just the president who decides the direction of our country. It is a collaborative process that permeates the federal, state, and local levels of government, from the White House to your town council or local alderman's office. You have the right to be part of the process and help shape the future.

CHAPTER 4

CONGRESS

"Although the job of a congressman involves several different roles, the main ones are as representative and legislator."
—Lee Hamilton

"Let us not seek the Republican answer or the Democratic answer, but the right answer. Let us not seek to fix blame for the past. Let us accept our own responsibility for the future."
—John F. Kennedy

With the constant barrage of political analysis and commentary, you might assume that most Americans today are well informed as to what each branch of government does. Yet, many Americans seem to lack a foundational understanding of the responsibilities of each branch of government, much to the frustration (I imagine) of our elected officials. A recent example illustrates the point. Vice President Kamala Harris was being interviewed by a popular radio host. The host expressed frustration that two Democratic Senators, Joe Manchin and Kristin Sinema, would not be voting for the president's proposed "Build Back Better" policy.

The host pointedly asked the vice president: "I want to know who the real president of this country is? Is it Joe Biden or Joe Manchin?" No doubt, the radio host knows that President Biden is the president. However, the role of the president and the responsibilities of members of Congress is likely less clear to many Americans.

The Vice President appeared perplexed by the question and perhaps irritated. She promptly ended the interview, but I can imagine she was tempted to remind the host of the role of the president, the role of the legislature, and the checks and balances between them.

It's easy to get carried away by rhetoric during presidential elections as the candidates emphatically tell us all the things they will do to make our lives better. They will "fix" healthcare or they will "empower unions." In reality, however, outside of a limited set of powers to sign executive orders, the president can't really do any of those things. It has to be the Congress who proposes and passes legislation to address those issues. The president's role is to sign the legislation into law…or veto it if he does not support it.

All branches of our federal government are designed to be separate but equal. Therefore, it is not accurate to say that one branch is more important than another. However, the legislative branch is the one responsible for making laws, so clearly its role is pretty important. The legislative branch was established by Article I of the Constitution and consists of both chambers of Congress—the House of Representatives and the Senate. Based on the Constitution, Congress has sole authority to enact legislation and declare war, the right to confirm or reject presidential appointments, and the authority to exercise significant investigative powers. That's why you will sometimes see corporate and military leaders, government officials, academic thought leaders and others called before a Congressional Committee to answer questions about topics of interest. The president has no such powers.

The House of Representatives has 435 elected members, one from each district in each state in our country. The number of representatives a state has depends on the state's population. There are also six non-voting members, representing the District of Columbia, the Commonwealth of Puerto Rico, and four other territories of the United States: American Samoa, Guam, the U.S. Virgin Islands, and the Northern Mariana Islands. The presiding officer of the chamber is the Speaker of the House and he or she is third in line to the president, just after the vice president. The Speaker is elected by the Representatives and is always a member of the majority party in the House.

The Senate is comprised of 100 senators. Unlike the House of Representatives, each state has only two senators, regardless of that state's population. Senators serve six-year terms that are staggered, so about one-third of the Senate is up for reelection every two years. The Vice President of the United States serves as President of the Senate and may cast the deciding vote in the event of a tie in the Senate.

The Senate has the sole power to confirm presidential appointments that require consent. However, the House must also approve appointments to the Vice Presidency. Importantly, the Senate also bears responsibility to try impeachment cases for federal officials referred to it by the House.

In order for the president to sign a piece of legislation into law, it must first be passed by both the House and the Senate. If the president vetoes a bill, Congress can override the veto by passing the bill again in each chamber with at least two-thirds of each body voting in favor.[xxi] This is why in cases where one or both chambers of Congress know they will not secure the required number of votes to pass a piece a legislation, they will often not bring it to a vote at all.

Approval Ratings—A Double-Edged Sword

When I mentioned Representative Ocasio-Cortez earlier, it's highly likely that you knew her name before I mentioned it. It's also probable that due to the enormous amount of media attention she commands, you have formed an opinion about her based on your perceptions and information you receive from your preferred media outlets. Yet, it would be easy to assume that she is likely not overly concerned about your opinions. Nor would it seem that she would worry about her overall approval ratings. Truth is that only registered voters in her own district (those who actually come in to vote) will decide whether she keeps her congressional seat. Senators have a somewhat higher burden to bear, as they must concern themselves with the views of registered voters across their entire state. No doubt, representing a politically homogenous district is a lot easier than trying to balance the competing interests and priorities in a politically heterogeneous state.

So why would a Congresswoman from a small district in New York care at all about what Texans in her Twitter mentions have to say about her? Ultimately, a national profile matters immensely to members of the legislative branch as most of them seek to not only keep their seat, but to be assigned to prestigious committee assignments and/or higher office. Not all elected officials desire to be President of the United States, but certainly many of them do. So, don't assume that your opinion, positive or negative, is meaningless simply because you don't live in a particular candidate's district or state. It is entirely possible that in the years to come, that young politician will be asking for your vote in a national election.

Why No Congressional Term Limits?

After the death of President Franklin D. Roosevelt, Congress passed the 22nd Amendment, which stated that no person will serve more than two four-year terms as president. This, of course, was after President Roosevelt served an unprecedented four terms in office. However, the 22nd Amendment only applies to the president, not to the Legislative branch. Why the omission?

There's a short, easy answer to this question. For term limits to apply to members of Congress, members of Congress have to be the ones to vote it into law. Reasonable minds would agree that scenario is unlikely, even if it is in the best interest of our country. Most people prefer stability in their professional careers and our elected representatives are no different. Yet, the weight of evidence suggests that most voters do not favor the current system, which does not impose term limits on members of Congress. In fact, over 60% of Americans support term limits, regardless of their party affiliation.[xxii] Yet, no bill to implement congressional term limits has been brought to the floor of either chamber.

However, in 2021, a group of Republicans introduced a constitutional amendment to limit the terms of House members to three 2-year terms and senators to two 6-year terms. But, like prior efforts to implement terms limits, the proposal has not gained meaningful traction. Part of this is because in 1995, the Supreme Court ruled it would require a Constitutional amendment, not simply passing a law to enforce term limits. Constitutional amendments require a two-thirds super majority vote in both chambers, not a simple majority, thus making it harder to pass than a typical law. This is by design, as the founders wanted to guard against impulsive changes to the Constitution. As James Madison noted in Federalist No. 58, the requirement for a super majority vote is a "shield to some particular interest, and another obstacle generally to hasty and partial measures."

Without a constitutional amendment, members of Congress can serve an unlimited number of terms, unless they are otherwise voted out of office. And that is the way they like it. Why wouldn't they? A history of voter apathy, when combined with political maneuvering and controversial practices such as gerrymandering, increases the likelihood that members of Congress will be able to retain their seats for as long as they want them.

Gerrymandering

Have you ever looked at a map of congressional districts? It's quite a mess, isn't it? A naive person might assume that the different sizes and shapes of congressional districts reflects population differences. That view is not just naïve, it is plain wrong.

Gerrymandering is the practice of manipulating boundaries of congressional districts to favor one party over another. To be sure, this is a practice that both Democrats and Republicans strategically employ. It's simple: it is easier to get a candidate elected to office if most people in that weirdly drawn district happens to be members of that candidate's political party. Nowadays, when you watch the news leading up to an election, the polished political analyst will inevitably be standing in front of a map of states or districts, each colored red, blue, or purple. Do you wonder how they can predict which way the vote will go *before* the votes are cast? Gerrymandering is partly why.

This practice is especially impactful to majority-African American communities because they predictably vote for Democratic candidates. As a result, African American communities are a particularly tempting target when a political party seeks to gerrymander in its favor.

> *"Typically, the goal in [packing minorities into a district] is not to reduce minority representation in the adjacent districts; it's to reduce [one party's] representation in those districts," said Nicholas Stephanopoulos, a professor at the University of Chicago Law School.*

> *Consider an example: Imagine the minority-favored candidate can win an election in a district if at least 30 percent of voters are minorities. What harm is done by the legislators packing the district up to 50 percent minority voters?*

> *Much like political gerrymandering, it limits black influence in surrounding districts. It would require the creation of, for instance, a 50 percent and a 10 percent black district, rather than two 30 percent black districts. In other words, the requirement would give black voters one representative of their choice rather than two.[xxiii]*

Opponents of gerrymandering argue that isolating votes into smaller and ever-more strangely shaped districts to keep a consistent voting block for a political party is not good for the country or for Americans looking to vote their interests. But it is good for the Democrat and Republican National Committees, who get to carve out their districts every ten years.

After each census population count, the number of congressional seats is apportioned based on the most recent population data. If a population in a certain area shrinks, then that district may be removed, and its communities are re-aligned to other districts. States are required to define and delineate their own congressional districts for the purpose of electing members to the House of Representatives. Each congressional district is expected to be equal in population to all other congressional districts in a state, so the state authorities of each party often get creative to find the appropriate number of people that largely share party affiliation.

Do you think gerrymandering isn't a big deal? As of 2018, partisan gerrymandering continued to exist in 35 states, while 15 states now require independent or neutral commissions to execute the redistricting process. Even today, political and legal battles centered on gerrymandering and the redistricting process are occurring all across the country as we head into the 2022 midterm elections. The Brennan Center for Justice recently opined that "as of February 16, 2022, a total of 50 cases have been filed challenging congressional and legislative maps in 19 states as racially discriminatory and/or partisan gerrymanders..."[xxiv] Clearly, gerrymandering is still a big deal but it, by no means, is the only hot topic of intense debate.

Campaign Finance

Regardless of your opinion of former President Trump, he made a promise on the campaign trail that had broad appeal. Specifically, he pledged to fund his own campaign and stated that he would not be beholden to special interests once he was in office. That message seemed to resonate with many voters.

It costs an enormous amount of money to run for national office and candidates typically receive financial support from corporations and political action committees (PACs), all of which have expectations for a quid pro quo, of sorts once their funded candidate is in office. This is a major reason why many people don't run for public office and why campaign promises to the general public often end up not being fulfilled. The vast majority of Americans would agree that the influence of money in politics is a problem. But what is anyone doing about it?

There have been several attempts at campaign finance reform, starting with the Tillman Act in 1907, which was designed to stop corporations from making political contributions. We all know how that turned out. The Federal Corrupt Practices Act in 1925 was far more successful in its aim to set contribution limits and the 1971 Federal Election Campaign Act (FECA) required corporations to disclose how much money they contributed to political candidates. There were several other legislative efforts, including the McCain-Feingold Act in 2002, which were intended to ban "soft money" donations to political parties. However, in the case of *Citizens United vs. Federal Election Commission,* the Supreme Court invalidated many of the previous attempts at campaign finance reform. The Court held that "corporations are people" and prohibited the government from placing limitations on the amount of campaign contributions corporations can make.

Ironically, the Citizens United ruling spurred the creation of PACs, which can raise amounts of money far exceeding what an individual candidate can solicit and spend it on campaign efforts such as advertising. This gives a firm advantage to candidates who are most attractive to corporations and other "big money" interests, as opposed to candidates who must rely primarily on grassroots support. After all, an individual is limited to donating just $2,900 per election to candidates, while no such limit is imposed on the amount of money a Super PAC can raise from corporations, unions, or individuals.

Super PACs do not make contributions directly to candidates; however, they influence the political process by financing independent expenditures and political activities in support of their preferred candidates. We have all seen political advertisements on television that place one candidate in a favorable light, while attacking the character, ethics, or competence of the opponent. Those advertisements are not always created or paid for by the candidate themselves; it is quite possible that it is the influence of a Super PAC.

What does this mean for the 80 Percent?

Regardless of your preferred party affiliation, it is in your interest to ask candidates questions about their position on gerrymandering, term limits, and campaign finance ethics. Their answers can be illuminating and help you make an informed decision about which candidate most closely aligns with your values. Viewed in isolation, these individual issues have not historically been foundational pillars on platforms for candidates from either party because they are not the issues that drive voter turnout. Nonetheless, it is important to inquire.

Submit your questions at town hall events. Write to the candidate's campaign headquarters or their office if the candidate already holds elected office. Knowing that these topics are important to their constituents can spark conversations. And, if those conversations become loud enough and frequent enough, they can also inspire change.

It is true that a single member of Congress cannot change the way campaign finances are run, or get a constitutional amendment passed regarding term limits. Furthermore, one person certainly can't standardize the congressional districting in your state. But it is important to remember what I said earlier: many members of Congress and other elected officials aspire to higher office, whether that be the presidency, perhaps the Supreme Court, a leadership role in the House or Senate, or some other powerful position in the political arena. Ensuring that your voice is heard at all levels of government may inspire the type of change you wish to see. In theory, the more power an elected official accumulates over the course of their career, the greater the influence they will have to drive the substantive changes you elected them to make in the first place.

CHAPTER 5
THE PRESIDENCY

*"All modern U.S. Presidents are perforce politicians, prisoners of their
past pronouncements, their party, their constituency,
and their colleagues."*

—Tony Judt

The executive branch is the largest branch in our government and is tasked with carrying out and enforcing laws. It includes the president, vice president, the Cabinet, executive departments, independent agencies, and a host of other boards, commissions, and committees.

The president is our head of state, leader of the federal government, and Commander in Chief of the armed forces. As we discussed in the previous chapter, the president serves a four-year term and can be elected no more than two times, thanks to the twenty-second amendment.

The vice president supports the president and is expected to step into the office of the president, fulfilling the duties of the chief executive, in the event the president becomes incapacitated or is otherwise unable to serve. The vice president can be elected and serve an unlimited number of four-year terms, even under a different president. It is an unlikely scenario, but if they chose, every president could have the same vice president, year after year.

The Cabinet advises the president. Cabinet members include the vice president, heads of executive departments, and other high-ranking government officials. Cabinet members are nominated by the president and must be approved by a simple majority of the Senate—51 votes, if all 100 senators vote. Unlike federal employees of departments and agencies, cabinet members serve at the president's pleasure and may be relieved of duty at any time.

Executive branch agencies, commissions, and committees perform much of the work done by the executive branch. The size of executive departments and independent agencies is what makes the executive branch of government the largest. And there are a number of them, including the Department of Defense, Department of State, Department of Justice, Department of Revenue, Department of Health and Human Services, Department of Education, Department of Veterans Affairs, Department of Agriculture, Department of Energy...and on and on it goes. You get the point. It will likely come as no surprise that the Department of Defense is the largest executive department with nearly three million employees. The largest annual budget? Well, that distinction currently goes to the Department of Health and Human Services. Its 2022 budget was roughly $1.6 trillion. Most entities you interact with in the federal government fall under the executive branch.

A bit of context about the executive branch and executive orders is worth sharing. Because federal agencies fall under the executive branch, the president was able to sign an executive order during the Covid-19 pandemic mandating vaccines for federal employees in these agencies. However, the president was not able to impose the same mandate on members of Congress and employees of the legislative branch, or the Supreme Court for that matter. The executive branch has no authority over the other branches of government, so the reach of presidential executive orders are limited to the executive branch.

The Evolution of Presidential Powers

Since the United States was founded, the role of the president has changed dramatically. As noted, when the founders first envisioned the presidency, the duties of the president were prescribed. However, those prescribed duties were certainly not all-encompassing. George Washington was trusted as a man of honor, thus his actions and behavior set the expectations of his successors. That meant it was more tradition than prescription in terms of what the president was expected to do (or not do).

That left the door open for a gradual expansion of the president's powers, driven largely by the country's needs during wartime.

Well, what happened was, in various wars, America needed to move quickly, and they needed one person to act on behalf of the entire Union. Well, there's only one person who can do that. But as people wanted quick action, they handed over more power to the president. Congress, which used to fight with the president a lot, during the Second World War and then on into our present day, has given up a lot of its power to the president. One of the key ones being the power to make war. Presidents can now go and make war. Well, that's not the original way it was arranged. And they've done it because there is a hunger in the country for quick action, but the problem and challenge of that is, if you invest somebody with power to do things quickly in an emergency, they hold on to that power and they don't let it go, and that means that they start doing things when it's not an emergency, that is then not vetted by the American system. And that system has both the judiciary and the legislative branch which are meant to hold back a president who's trying to act too quickly and do too much.[xxv]

It may surprise you to know the United States has not declared war since World War II. But what about Korea and Vietnam? What about the intervention in Kosovo? What about the twenty-year quagmire in Iraq and Afghanistan? If those weren't wars, what were they?

Those are technically conflicts, which is a neat sidestep around the fact that presidents officially cannot declare war. But they can order our military troops to address conflicts. And presidents don't require bipartisan support to do so.

To be clear, the expanded powers were not usurped by power-hungry presidents. Rather, these powers were willingly relinquished by the other branches of government, specifically the legislative branch. It used to be that members of Congress were the key actors in American politics, but that has certainly changed over the years. Now the president is front and center, and it is the president's face and voice that is associated with every major decision—both popular and unpopular. If a decision turns out to be unpopular with the American public, well, the president can only serve two terms anyway. On the other hand, a member of Congress can, in theory, serve for life unless voted out of office. So, it should come as no surprise that members of Congress so willingly surrender some of their responsibilities to the president.

American politics has created a situation, and television has made this so much worse, where people run for office promising the sun, the moon, and the stars. Donald Trump, when he was running, said "I alone can fix it." That is not the way the country was originally founded. That one person could fix or unfix things. It was supposed to be a country with representatives of the entire country. But politics has created a system where, whether it's a Republican or Democrat, they run by saying I can do anything. Well, that means when you get in the office you want those quick powers that allow you to keep those campaign promises, and those quick powers are only quick if Congress and the courts aren't in the way. So, politics and the way you run for office makes presidents want to have every possible power at their disposal.[xxvi]

Notwithstanding the amount of power that has been relinquished to the office of the presidency, what are the qualities Americans want to see in their president? A poll conducted by Yahoo News/ YouGovAmerica concluded that more than any other quality, Americans want their president to take responsibility.[xxvii] In fact, more than 80% of Democrats and Republicans agree. Similarly, a significant majority of Republicans and Democrats value competence and honesty. Republicans, however, value strength more than Democrats, while more Democrats believe empathy is an important quality. Interestingly, neither party viewed audacity as a quality our president must possess. So, it would seem that no matter how much power has been entrusted to a president, a substantial majority of Americans agree that character matters.

What Does This Mean for the Voters?

For most Americans, debates about the separation of powers are likely not a trending topic on social media or even a focal point of discussions at dinner parties. However, only 36% of Democrats and Democratic-leaning independents and only 9% of Republicans and Republican-leaning independents say they can trust government.[xxviii] So, what's the problem? The data is clearly telling us that character matters and we do not trust our elected officials.

One has to wonder if that rising distrust is attributable to the expanding powers of the president, the president's heavy reliance on executive orders, congressional tribalism, petty politics, legislative gridlock, or the alarming rate in which alleged government scandals are reported. Voters would be wise to pay attention and conduct research on candidates running for public office. Do they make promises on the campaign trail that you know they cannot fulfill? Do they express an opinion about reducing or expanding the power of the presidency? If so, do those statements align with your values? It may not be a hot topic on social media, but it is an important one that impacts the balance of power in our nation's capital and strikes at the heart of our democracy.

CHAPTER 6
THE SUPREME COURT

"The Supreme Court's only armor is the cloak of public trust; its sole ammunition, the collective hope of our society."
—Irving R. Kaufman

In chapter five, we discussed how the role of the legislative branch has evolved during the last thirty years. What was initially designed to be the most powerful and influential branch of government has, over time, abdicated much of its power to the other branches. As noted, it relinquished some of its powers to the president and the agencies of the executive branch. Other powers have been absorbed by the judicial branch, and specifically the Supreme Court, which is the highest court of the land. As the role of the president and Congress has evolved, so too has the role of the Supreme Court over the course of its history.

History of the Court

Congress established the Supreme Court in 1789 with the passage of the Judiciary Act. Although the Constitution described in great detail the powers, structure, and functions of the legislative and executive branches of government, it was by design less prescriptive in defining the roles and responsibilities of the judicial branch. Ultimately it was left to Congress to determine the role and powers of the Supreme Court. The only guiding language from the Constitution was that judicial power be "vested in one supreme court, and in such inferior

Courts as the Congress may from time to time ordain and establish."

As the nation's highest court, the Supreme Court operates as an appellate body, rendering final judgment on lower courts' decisions. It also acts as the arbiter of cases involving the constitutionality of laws, disputes between states or between citizens of different states, and in cases of maritime jurisdiction. Only in these instances does the Supreme Court have original jurisdiction, meaning it serves as the trial court, not the appellate court. In those cases, the Chief Justice oversees the trial. Note, however, that only a small fraction of cases are argued in trials before the Supreme Court. Most cases argued before the Supreme Court are based on actions appealing lower court decisions.[xxix]

Currently, there are nine Supreme Court Justices— Chief Justice John Roberts, Jr., Clarence Thomas, Samuel A. Alito, Sonia Sotomayor, Elena Kagan, Neil Gorsuch, Brett Kavanaugh, Amy Coney Barrett, and Ketanji Brown-Jackson. Justice Brown-Jackson recently succeeded Justice Stephen G. Breyer who retired June 30, 2022. With her appointment to the Court, Justice Brown-Jackson became the fifth woman appointed to the Supreme Court in its 233-year history and the first African American woman to serve on the Court.

For historical context, Justice Sandra Day O'Connor holds the honor of being the first woman Supreme Court Justice. She was nominated by Republican President Ronald Reagan and served on the court from 1981–2006. Prior to Judge Ketanji Brown-Jackson's nomination, there have only been two African American Supreme Court Justices, the first of which was Justice Thurgood Marshall. He was nominated by Democratic President Lyndon B. Johnson and served on the court from 1967–1991. This context is important because the diversity of gender, race, and thought that the court currently enjoys is the product of a process that started over fifty years ago with contributions from Republicans and Democrats. That fact sometimes gets lost in modern-day rhetoric. But, I digress...

The Supreme Court has not always been comprised of nine Justices. When it was originally formed in 1789, the court was comprised of six Justices. In 1807, a seventh Justice was added, followed by an eighth and a ninth in 1837, and a tenth in 1863. You likely have heard recent debates on the news about "court packing," but the number of Supreme Court Justices has always been a politically-charged topic. The number of Justices was changed to nine because President Lincoln "packed the court" to ensure his anti-slavery measures were successful. The original seven Justices on the Supreme Court were not all inclined to support President Lincoln, so he appointed two new Justices, tipping the scales in his favor.[xxx]

After President Lincoln's death in 1866, Congress voted to allow the gradual reduction of the court back to seven Justices, thus as Justices died or retired, they would not be replaced. This was in recognition of the fact that President Lincoln had taken extraordinary measures during wartime. At least that was the stated reason. However, the real motivation behind the move was to prevent President Andrew Johnson from appointing a new Justice. President Johnson was largely unpopular and was eventually impeached in 1868 (though narrowly acquitted) for allegedly violating the Tenure of Office Act, which was designed to prohibit a sitting president from removing cabinet officials without Senate consent.

Following President Johnson's tenure, Congress adopted new legislation in 1869 that set the number of Justices at nine, where it has remained ever since. However, there have certainly been subsequent attempts to change the number of Justices. For instance, Democratic President Franklin D. Roosevelt asked Congress to allow him to appoint an additional Justice for each member of the court aged seventy years or older who refused to retire, an obvious political move, similar to those employed by Presidents Lincoln and Johnson. However, his request was denied and the number of Justices remained at nine.

The Constitution gives the president the right to make appointments to the Supreme Court and to the lower federal courts "with the advice and consent of the Senate." Once the president nominates his or her preferred candidate, the Senate Judiciary Committee will then conduct hearings on the nomination to the Supreme Court, and a simple majority of the full Senate is required for confirmation. Since the members of the Supreme Court are given a lifetime appointment, they may only be removed from their position through the impeachment process, ending with a conviction by the Senate. Only one Justice has ever been impeached. That distinction goes to Justice Samuel Chase. He was impeached in 1805 in connection with two politically-sensitive cases in which he was accused of refusing to dismiss biased jurors and unjustly taking adverse actions against defense witnesses. Ultimately, however, Justice Chase was acquitted by the Senate.

The Supreme Court is unique among appellate courts in that it has almost exclusive discretion in deciding which cases it will hear and how many cases it will place on its docket. That said, the Supreme Court typically hears about one hundred cases per term (October through June of each year). That may sound like a lot, but it is not when you consider that it typically receives 5,000 – 10,000 requests per term. This massive number of requests is a relatively recent phenomenon and reflects a fivefold increase from the 1940s. Of course, the U.S. population has grown since that time, but Americans have also become increasingly litigious and ever more reliant on the judicial process, rather than the legislative process, to resolve disputes and identify potential remedies for alleged wrongdoing and damages.

Expansion of Power and Importance

Though we will have an entire chapter devoted to the issue of abortion later in the book, a discussion of the role of the Supreme Court cannot be undertaken without examining the watershed case of Roe vs. Wade.

Part of the reason every Supreme Court nomination takes such an ugly turn is because of the implications it could have on the Roe vs. Wade ruling. In 1973, the Supreme Court held that the right to abortion is a constitutional right, thus making the procedure legal in all fifty states and in U.S. territories, regardless of the wishes of the residents and legislators of those states.

This highly-contentious ruling resulted in a feeling of empowerment for its proponents, giving them a new sense that the judiciary, not the legislature, would be the preferred path to get their causes recognized under the law. Meanwhile, opponents of Roe vs. Wade felt betrayed and alarmed, spawning the terminology "activist judges" for the first time. No longer was the Supreme Court viewed as a neutral arbiter of existing law, but just another political body.

In addition, Roe v. Wade accelerated an already increasing appeal to federal authority as opposed to state authority. Instead of activists working with their state legislators to pass laws, which is admittedly a lengthy process, they began filing legal proceedings against the state, typically arguing constitutional or civil rights violations.

In 2015, Obergefell vs. Hodges highlighted another controversial case that, in generations past, would have been a matter for state legislators to resolve rather than federal courts. In that case, the Supreme Court held that same-sex couples have the constitutional right to marry. With the ruling came the requirement for every state to legalize same-sex marriages, regardless of local opposition. There were several individual states that attempted to challenge the ruling but any proposed bans were deemed unconstitutional by the Supreme Court.[xxxi]

Though the Supreme Court, by necessity, declines to hear the majority of the cases it is petitioned to consider, the ones that do make it onto the docket often have the potential to impact the lives of millions of Americans.

The Left-Right Divide on the Supreme Court's Role

The great divide between the parties comes along with this question: should nine unelected judges serving a lifetime appointment have the right to make such weighty decisions? Is that their role? For Republicans and those who lean more toward an originalist view, the answer is decidedly no.

Take, for example, the question of marriage. For those of you who are married, do you remember getting your marriage license? Was it from a federal agency? No, it was from the state. Republicans argue that the question of marriage is not addressed in the constitution and therefore should not be a matter for federal courts. Rather, they generally contend that questions pertaining to the institution of marriage are more appropriately left to the jurisdiction of the individual states.

Additionally, many Republicans believe that marriage should not be regulated or overseen by the government at all. It is a religious ceremony, one binding a couple before a deity, sanctifying a union, and "allowing" them to form a family unit.

On the other hand, Democrats tend to view federal courts as an equalizer of sorts, a body that can right what they believe are unfair laws or unequal outcomes.

The Supreme Court performs a variety of functions, but the main one that people talk about is the power of constitutional review. The way this power works is the Supreme Court has the ability to declare laws as either allowed by the constitution or disallowed by the constitution. This is an extraordinary power that can be used to accomplish anything, whether good, bad or indifferent. You can use the power to say school segregation laws are disallowed (Brown (1954)) or to say that school desegregation laws are disallowed (Parents Involved (2007)). You can use it to say laws restricting voting rights are disallowed (Harper (1966)) or to say that the Voting Rights Act is disallowed (Shelby County (2013)). You can use it to say laws restricting contraception are disallowed (Griswold (1965)) or to say that laws requiring insurance to cover contraception are disallowed (Burwell (2014))...

Naturally, the sorting of laws into the disallowed or allowed buckets depends almost entirely on political ideology and therefore on the political composition of the court. If liberals are in control, they place socially conservative laws into the disallowed bucket and place progressive economic laws in the allowed bucket. If conservatives are in control — as they are currently and look like they will continue to be for a long time — they place progressive economic laws in the disallowed bucket and place socially conservative laws in the allowed bucket.[xxxii]

Shifting political ideologies have the potential to disrupt the status quo, with laws that affect people's lives swinging wildly from one election cycle to the next. Ultimately, which ideology prevails depends upon which party is in power, and which party's appointees hold sway on the Supreme Court.

The Impact of Lifetime Tenure

The majority of democracies around the world do not offer lifetime tenure for their high court appointees. Most often, they institute term limits or mandatory retirement ages. Why is the United States different?

Michael Meltsner, a Northeastern law professor who has spent much of his career focused on the Supreme Court, argues that the founders of the United States preferred lifetime tenure in order to protect Supreme Court Justices from partisan politics. "That was put into the Constitution to preserve the total independence of the judiciary," said Meltsner, the George J. and Kathleen Waters Matthews Distinguished University Professor of Law. "Once a Justice is confirmed and takes a seat on the court, they're not beholden to anybody."[xxxiii]

Unlike state and local judges who may be subject to elections and recalls if they run afoul of their constituents, Supreme Court Justices are able to make rulings that they understand will be unpopular without fear of losing their position on the bench. As a result, they should not feel pressure to bow to political interests and instead interpret the law and the Constitution without bias, undue influence, or conflicts of interest. At least, that was the idea...

Obviously, Supreme Court Justices are human, so they have their own political views and their own personal interests, which may in fact influence their decisions. As a result, there are often heated debates and polarized discourse whenever a president seeks to make a new appointment to the Supreme Court. Opponents of the appointing president understand that the Justice, if confirmed by the Senate, will remain on the court long after the president's tenure has ended. Even if every seat in both chambers of Congress is filled with opposing party members, that Justice will still have a say over the interpretation of laws in our country.

Periodically, debates about term limits for Justices surface in the media, just as it does for members of Congress. Such debates are typically raised for political reasons, but sometimes the debate focuses on the age of the Justices.

When the Constitution was written, the average life expectancy for men was less than fifty years, so there was limited impact from a lifetime appointment. Additionally, older people in political positions usually retired willingly well before death at that time.

However, things have changed. As of 2021, the average life expectancy in the U.S. was 78.99 years.[xxxiv] People are living almost three decades longer and are not retiring as early as they once may have. This includes our political class.

Changing demographics have led to intergenerational debates (e.g., Baby Boomers and the Silent Generation vs. Millennials and Gen Z) regarding the perceived refusal of older generations to retire and make room for younger Americans to advance up the corporate ranks[xxxv] and in politics.[xxxvi] There were some rumblings, in fact, that Justice Stephen Breyer did not actually wish to retire, that he was pressured to do so by activists and political actors.[xxxvii] They were apparently concerned that if Justice Breyer, at age 83, were to become incapacitated or die during a Republican administration, then that would tip the balance of the court for a generation or more. The motivation to end his tenure while President Biden was still in office was so great, apparently, that the announcement of his retirement was released before Justice Breyer was ready for it.[xxxviii]

The rush for a new, younger Justice might be understandable from a certain perspective. Consider, for example, that when Justice Amy Coney Barrett was confirmed in 2020, she was forty-eight years old. It is reasonable to assume that if she serves on the court for the remainder of her life (based on the average lifespan of a Caucasian woman), she may hold her seat for forty years. That is a very long time.

Another concern of an aging Supreme Court is the question of competence. Each person is different, and there can be no sweeping generalizations based on a person's age. However, it is an undeniable fact that our bodies (including our brains) deteriorate as we age. Thus, some have advocated for regular cognitive tests for public officials over a certain age.

Unlike most other issues, skepticism regarding lifetime appointment of Justices is not a partisan issue, and opinions vary across the political spectrum. However, changing the current system would require a constitutional amendment, which appears unlikely in the near future. Nonetheless, it is important to understand the views of each Supreme Court nominee. Once confirmed, their views will influence and impact our lives for many years.

CHAPTER 7

ENTITLEMENTS

*"You cannot help men permanently by doing for them what
they should do for themselves."*
—President Abraham Lincoln

Social Security

Part of President Roosevelt's New Deal was the Social Security Act of 1935, which had several provisions, the most well-known of which was the creation of a retired workers fund. Prior to the passage of the Social Security Act, American workers could retire only if they had saved enough money during their working years or had family members who were willing and able to support them. As you can imagine, most working-class people were unable to save enough for retirement, especially those who were injured or disabled due to the dangerous nature of their jobs. The Act allowed workers aged sixty-five or older to receive a stipend from their job, medical benefits in the form of Medicare (which we will discuss later in this chapter), and to receive survivorship benefits for a deceased spouse.[xxxix]

The Act required all working adults to pay into a Social Security trust fund, ensuring money was available for the elderly as they retired. Ideally, a person who paid into the fund during their working years would not have to rely on family members during retirement, nor fear being cast into poverty, even if they didn't earn or save enough money to have their own retirement account. Additionally, Social Security was designed to provide income benefits for those who are permanently disabled and unable to work.

You will not find many legislators or citizens on either side of the political divide who espouse abolishing the Social Security system (though you might inevitably find a few). However, Social Security, as it is currently constructed and implemented, does have its detractors. Today, Social Security accounts for roughly $939 billion, or 24%, of the federal budget. Clearly, it has major implications not only for retirees but for our country to meet its national priorities.

Opposition to Social Security is most often attributable to generational imbalances in the current system. Specifically, the payout rates retirees currently enjoy are believed to be unsustainable. Based on estimates in February 2022, the Social Security trust fund's reserves will be depleted in 2034.[xl] In the absence of changes to the current system, this means that everyone who retires in 2034 or after will be forced to receive reduced benefits, even though they paid into the system at the full rate. How could this be? It is a fair question that many Americans have asked.

As a starting point, it is important to understand that contributions to the Social Security trust fund are not sequestered in their own account for the exclusive use of Social Security payments. The contributions deducted from your paycheck may be used to fund any and all federal programs. Your contributions are shown as a separate line item on your pay statement, but not necessarily allocated for use in that way.

"It is all predicated on money going in from current workers to money going out to beneficiaries," says Kathleen Romig, a Senior Policy Analyst at the Center on Budget and Policy Priorities. "You want to have the worker to beneficiary ratio at a sort of healthy level where you do not have too few [working] people paying for too many beneficiaries."

Over the next ten plus years, the Social Security administration will draw down its reserves as a decreasing number of workers will be paying for an increasing number of beneficiaries. This is due to a decline in the birth rate after the baby boom period that took place right after World War II, from 1946 to 1964.

"People are having fewer children and because the birth rate is declining you just have fewer workers paying for beneficiaries," says Romig.

Starting in 2034, the Social Security administration will run out of the excess reserves it has and will only be able to pay out a portion of a retiree's full benefits — 78% to be exact. This means that retirees could receive reduced monthly benefits or fewer checks each year, according to Romig — that is, unless there is a policy change made by the U.S. government.[xli]

Faced with such dire prospects, some legislators (most frequently, Republicans) are questioning whether the government should be in the business of funding retirement accounts at all, especially for Americans who are able to save for retirement through an employer-sponsored 401k plan, individual retirement account (IRA), or otherwise. A possible solution to the Social Security trust fund shortfall involves means testing, which would place a limit on who could receive Social Security benefits starting at age sixty-five. One popular proposal would permit Social Security payments only to those who earned an average of $49,000 per year or less. While this would ensure that those who need it most would receive benefits, the problem arises when you understand that Social Security benefits are not bestowed on the American people as a gift. It is a right earned by American workers who have made contributions to the trust fund over the course of their careers. It would not be well received by the American public if they were told: "We will take money from your paycheck every two weeks to fund retirement. But not your retirement."

Consider earning an average of $65,000 a year, which is hardly considered wealthy by most standards. Yet, under some popular proposals, Americans with that level of income would be entirely responsible for their own retirement needs while simultaneously being required to fund the retirement needs of others. As you can imagine, such proposals do not sit well with most Americans.

How you feel about Social Security and what should be done to revamp the existing system (it *must* be revamped, one way or another) depends on how much responsibility you believe the government has for your well-being. It is important to evaluate your elected officials for their opinion on the matter, whether they believe it is the government's duty to provide a minimum benefit for all Americans, or only certain Americans based on need. For some issues in this book, it may be hard to pin down legislators on their views, as the problem may be abstract or perceived as a "someday but not today" problem. Social Security, unfortunately, is not one of those issues. We can no longer "kick the can down the road" as the expression goes. So if you are considering a candidate running for office, be sure to find out their stance on Social Security.

Healthcare

Of the many issues that divide our country, few are as complicated as the debate over healthcare. The U.S. has some of the most advanced healthcare capabilities in the world. However, gaining access to healthcare can be difficult for those who lack health insurance or perhaps even those with insurance…just not the right kind.

As of 2021, 9.6 percent of Americans were uninsured[xlii] and that does not consider those who are underinsured. As a result, many Americans do not receive the healthcare they need. For those who have access, the cost of healthcare can often be financially devastating. The healthcare industry accounts for roughly one-sixth of the U.S. economy, and Americans spend more money on healthcare than any other country in the world.[xliii] According to the *American Journal of Medicine*, medical debt is the biggest cause of bankruptcy with 62% of bankruptcies in America being caused by high healthcare costs.[xliv]

The U.S. does have healthcare programs such as Medicare and Medicaid, which are designed to serve as a social safety net of sorts to assist Americans in need. These programs can help mitigate the risk of bankruptcy attributable to exorbitant healthcare costs, especially in cases of catastrophic injury or illness. Today, Medicare, Medicaid, and other healthcare costs account for roughly $1.1 trillion, or 27%, of the federal budget.

Medicaid & Medicare

Both Medicare and Medicaid are government-funded insurance programs, but they have different eligibility requirements and coverage benefits. Medicare was signed into law with the Social Security Act, ensuring those over age sixty-five would be able to access medical care. Today, there are several types of Medicare that senior citizens have access to, including Part A (hospital care), Part B (office visits), and Part D (prescriptions). Medicare provides an important benefit to seniors; however, it is not a catch-all, which is why private insurance companies sell Medicare supplemental policies.

Medicaid was signed into law in 1965 in response to the rising cost of private healthcare services. Medicaid is available in all states, territories, and the District of Columbia and is generally designed to provide health coverage for low-income Americans. While Medicare is fully funded by the federal government, Medicaid costs are shared by federal and state governments. This is an important distinction because Medicaid eligibility requirements and benefits may differ depending on which state you reside in.

Affordable Care Act

In 2010, President Obama signed into law the Affordable Health Care Act (ACA). Nicknamed "Obamacare," this multi-year rollout program resulted in a 17.5 million decrease in uninsured Americans between 2010 and 2019.[xlv] One of the most notable provisions in the ACA is that it prevented insurance companies from denying coverage to people based on pre-existing conditions. Prior to the ACA, it is estimated that one in seven Americans were denied health insurance because of a pre-existing condition.

Opponents of the ACA argued that it did not lower the cost of healthcare. In fact, insurance costs increased significantly for some Americans. Many Republicans staunchly opposed the ACA on the grounds that it disempowered patients while increasing government bureaucracy. Some provisions were even escalated to the Supreme Court, most notably the ACA's mandate for all Americans to purchase health insurance. Opponents of the legislation argued that the mandate was an unconstitutional tax on American citizens. The Supreme Court rejected that argument in 2021, leaving the ACA in effect.[xlvi]

After President Donald Trump was elected in 2016, there were several attempts by the Republican-majority Congress to repeal and replace the ACA. However, this has been proven to be a difficult task as the healthcare system is extremely complex. One notable bill that was proposed but eventually rejected was the Cassidy-Graham Bill, which sought to repeal the ACA's mandate to purchase health insurance. In addition, it proposed to eliminate the expansion of Medicaid and middle-class subsidies intended to offset the cost of insurance.

Healthcare reform is a controversial issue, which highlights fundamental differences between Republicans and Democrats. In general, Republicans view the ACA as an attempt by the government to gain more power and control over the American people by imposing a European-style bureaucracy to manage all aspects of Americans' lives. Concerns about government intrusion in healthcare decisions gained traction among many Americans, including Democratic voters following several high-profile cases in Britain. The most sensational of these cases involved Alfie Evans, a terminally-ill child who was denied an experimental, but potentially life-saving remedy by the United Kingdom's National Health System (NHS).

It was even more outrageous to many Americans that Alfie's parents were physically prevented from taking Alfie out of the hospital to a waiting airplane that would have taken the baby to Italy for surgery. Americans could understand a national healthcare service not providing funding for an experimental surgery. However, they were less understanding of why police were deployed to actively prevent another country from performing the surgery.[xlvii] The thought of a government exerting its power over a family's healthcare decisions for their child put a notable chill on enthusiasm for more government control over healthcare in the U.S., as did the subsequent lockdowns and restrictions that were imposed during the Covid-19 pandemic.

Many Democrats view universal healthcare as a basic human right. Based on that perspective, all Americans should have easy and quality access to it. However, debates about universal healthcare inevitably relate back to our previous discussion of positive rights versus negative rights. Ultimately, healthcare is a service that requires a person's labor. Therefore, Republicans are less inclined to recognize it as a basic human right. How can one person have a basic right to another person's time and labor?

On the other hand, Democrats question how we can call ourselves the greatest country in the world if our citizens are one major illness or accident away from bankruptcy. Yet, now that the ACA has been the law of the land for several years, both parties recognize its limitations, notwithstanding its good intentions.

With President Biden in office, it appears the ACA will continue to be the law of the land for the foreseeable future. Even though many Americans remain opposed to the requirement to purchase health insurance,[xlviii] our current system is so complicated that it is doubtful a replacement will be conceived in the near term. Two alternatives that are often discussed involve (i) a complete government takeover of healthcare (like Great Britain's NHS), or and (ii) the abolishment of insurance and the transition of healthcare to the open market.

Both alternatives are objectively terrifying to most Americans, especially those with chronic health issues or children with special needs. Therefore, neither proposal has garnered meaningful support. Yet, most Americans agree that our current system is not ideal. If it is to be improved, it will require demands from the voting public and serious, bipartisan efforts to reform our healthcare apparatus.

Health and the African American Community

African Americans face the greatest health risks of all ethnic groups in the United States.[xlix] This may surprise you, but it shouldn't. The weight of evidence suggests that poor health and lower economic standing is inextricably linked. To that end, African Americans have the lowest median household income in the United States, at just $45,870 in 2020.[l] As a result, African Americans are more likely to rely on public health insurance programs such as Medicaid in order to access affordable healthcare. The African American population is also more strongly concentrated in southern states, which generally offer less generous Medicaid benefits. Furthermore, many of those southern states have not implemented the ACA's Medicare expansion. Even in states that have implemented the Medicare expansion, African Americans often fall within a coverage gap—meaning they earn too much income to qualify for the traditional Medicaid program, but not enough income to qualify for premium tax credits under marketplace plans.[li]

Health disparities between African Americans and their white counterparts are not a new phenomenon. It is an issue that has plagued our nation since its founding and both Democratic and Republican administrations have implemented measures to improve outcomes. As previously discussed, Democratic President Lyndon B. Johnson signed into law the Medicare and Medicaid Act of 1965. Yet, it was Republican President Ronald Reagan who championed the creation of the Office of Minority Health in 1986, with a stated mission to eliminate health disparities and improve the health of minorities.

In 1984, Margaret Heckler, then Secretary of Health and Human Services (HHS), dissatisfied with the way health disparities were being reported to Congress, provided the first comprehensive review of health disparities endured by black and minority groups, compared with whites; the report laid the foundations for action to eliminate these disparities through health education, promotion, and access to health care. One of the most significant outcomes of the 1985 Report of the Secretary's Task Force on Black and Minority Health, also known as the Heckler Report, was the creation of the Office of Minority Health in 1986, with the mission "to improve the health of racial and ethnic minority populations through the development of health policies and programs that will eliminate health disparities." The Heckler Report called health disparities among minority groups an affront both to our ideals and to the ongoing genius of American medicine.[lii]

At present, the top three causes of death for African Americans are heart diseases, cancer, and Covid-19. What is striking, however, is that according to the Center for Disease Control (CDC), African Americans make up 13% of the U.S. population, yet account for 23% of Covid-19 deaths.[liii] Furthermore, the Office of Minority Health has indicated that African Americans carry higher risk of heart disease, stroke, cancer, asthma, influenza and pneumonia, diabetes, and HIV/AIDs. Despite contributions from Democrats and Republicans, health disparities clearly remain and must be addressed to improve health outcomes for African Americans.

Ultimately, making quality healthcare more accessible for all Americans will require the combined efforts of our federal and state governments, private enterprise, and bipartisan support from Republicans and Democrats.

Education

In 2021, Virginia elected a new governor, Republican Glenn Youngkin. The election was notable because Virginia has tended to vote for Democratic gubernatorial candidates in recent years. In fact, since 2002, four of five governors elected during that period were Democrats. Furthermore, Democratic President Biden won the state of Virginia by a full ten percentage points in the 2020 presidential election. What caused this monumental shift? Perhaps there were multiple reasons, but the issue of education appears to have been the primary driver.

> *By late October, polls showed that voters considered education the most important issue in the race, and Democratic gubernatorial candidate Terry McAuliffe impaled himself on his own tongue by saying, "I do not think parents should be telling schools what they should teach."[liv]*

As it turned out, Virginians didn't much like being told that they should have no voice when it comes to matters of education. They were required to pay for public schools (whether their own children attended them or not), but had no say in the curriculum, extra-curricular activities, or the adult-centered books available in school libraries. Importantly, parents had no "right" to be notified when a violent crime had occurred on school grounds. Virginia parents did not like that at all and they voted accordingly.

The conflict in Virginia brought into sharp focus the fact that parents (i.e., voters) may have strong views about education that may not always align with the administration of our public school systems. Those views seemingly overrode any party loyalty those parents may have had in advance of election day.

School Choice

Virginia highlights only one example but there has been a growing movement among parents all over the country to (i) increase home-schooling, and (ii) advocate for school choice. Home-schooling is not a viable alternative for everyone, especially in single-parent and low-income homes, where adults in the household are likely working and may have multiple jobs. School choice, however, would not necessarily disrupt household employment dynamics.

So, what exactly is school choice? You may have heard it referred to as a school voucher program. The idea is that your tax dollars will follow your child to the school of your choice, whether public or private, rather than automatically being allocated to the public school district where you reside. Teachers' unions and public school bureaucracies disapprove of the school voucher program, in part, because it would potentially reduce the number of jobs in the public school system. There are multiple industries that receive state and federal tax dollars to perpetuate a broken system, but the public education system is among the most prominent, as the great majority of American children attend them during their formative years.

The school choice movement challenges lawmakers to re-examine traditional "residential assignment" for public education. Nearly 80% of American children attend schools in their assigned school district, while only 20% attend a different public school chosen by their parents. That should come as no surprise when you consider that not all public school districts accept transfers and not all families can accommodate the longer commute.

The ability of parents to choose their child's school is largely dependent on their income and financial resources. More specifically, they can choose to reside in a wealthy neighborhood with quality schools or pay the tuition and fees for a private school education. Over half of all homebuyers (both with and without children) take school district quality into consideration before making an offer to purchase. The great disparities that exist between the education wealthy children receive relative to their middle and lower-class counterparts is well-documented and goes back decades. It is the primary issue that fuels the school choice movement.

Another argument for school choice arose during the COVID lockdowns. Each school district has its own policies, usually informed by state and local ordinances, but not always. During the two years of COVID lockdowns and restrictions, there were significant disparities in the quality and consistency of children's education depending on the school they attended. "That means that in the same state, and even within the same school district, students living in neighboring attendance zones could have had radically different learning experiences."[lv]

The pandemic not only disrupted the public-school education experience, it also adversely impacted parents' ability to manage their households. For example, many parents were ordered back to work, but their children's school remained closed. Further, when schools were opened, parents sometimes received calls informing them that a student was experiencing Covid-19 symptoms, which required their children to quarantine at home. As a result, the parents may have had to leave work to be home with their children during the quarantine period.

Working parents found themselves in the untenable situation of having children who were in school yet also needed full-time childcare. Understandably, many working-class and middle-class parents simply could not afford the additional expense.

The uncertainty increased interest in school choice, as parents witnessed other nearby schools navigate through the pandemic more efficiently than their children's school, but found they were not allowed to transfer. Parents were understandably frustrated by declining learning outcomes, which were largely attributable to the lockdowns, challenges with online learning, and sporadic school attendance:

Like students throughout the country, state data show Humboldt County children saw their test scores take a hit in both math and English last year across grade levels. About 44.72% of students in the county met or exceeded the standard for their grade level in English and language arts in the 2018-2019 school year compared to 41.51% in 2020-2021. Similarly, the percentage of students that met or exceeded math standards dropped from 32.47% to 28.16% in the same time frame.

At the same time, the number of students who didn't meet the standard went from 31.37% in English and 38.31% in math before the pandemic to 31.73% in English and 42.23% in math during the 2020-2021 school year.[lvi]

Many parents began to ask: what, exactly, are we paying for? My child is not learning effectively. I am not able to go to work while my child is home. My child's mental and emotional health has suffered, and they are not prepared for the next grade level. Why then, am I forced to continue sending them to this specific public school?

Families, especially parents in low-income areas that do not have access to technology that makes online classes possible, should not feel trapped in assigned schools when school districts are closed to in-person learning. According to the Pew Research Center, 72 percent of parents in lower-

income brackets report being "very" or "somewhat" concerned this fall that their children are "falling behind in school as a result of the disruptions caused by the pandemic."[lvii]

Opponents of school choice note that voucher programs rarely provide students with full tuition to the best performing private schools. They argue that neither charter nor private schools are obligated to accept a particular student. Further, they allege that school vouchers will increase segregation by aiding "white flight" from the worst schools, which are generally minority-majority schools.

Proponents of school choice counter that vouchers are available for public and private schools. For instance, if School A suffers from poor test scores, high crime, and is generally failing, it should come as no surprise that School A students would want to attend school elsewhere. Some may choose to attend private schools or charter schools, while others may opt for another public school. Using private markets as a proxy, proponents of school choice contend that if a school is failing, then it shouldn't be in business. They argue that children should not be forced to accept an inferior or inadequate educational experience.

State of Schools in the African American Community

In 1960, it is estimated that roughly 23% of African Americans graduated high school compared to more than 40% of their White counterparts.[lviii] Some sixty years later, the U.S. has experienced a dramatic increase in high school graduation rates for all races, although African American graduation rates still lag many of their contemporaries. As of 2019, the high school graduation rate for African Americans has improved to 79.6%.[lix] By comparison, the graduation rate for Whites and Asians were 89.4% and 92.6%, respectively. No doubt, we have made progress, but we still have plenty of work to do.

"Waiting for Superman" was a 2010 documentary that detailed the stark reality for many African American children in poor neighborhoods, specifically the failing schools they attended and the resulting poor life outcomes that followed. The film showed parents clamoring every year for their children to be admitted into competitive charter schools that, like the local public schools, were majority-minority. The primary difference, however, was that the African American and other children of color that attended charter schools were thriving. Unfortunately, there is a limited number of available seats and charter schools typically hold a lottery to determine who will be admitted. As a result, parents must leave it up to chance whether their child will be accepted and afforded an opportunity to receive a quality education.

You wouldn't think that over six decades following the Supreme Court's landmark ruling in Brown v. Board of Education that American schools would still be so heavily segregated by race and produce strikingly different outcomes...but it is true. This reality is partly attributable to the residential public school mandate. It also highlights that majority African American neighborhoods are often socio-economically disadvantaged in comparison to majority-white neighborhoods.

The weight of evidence shows the lack of integration in schools for African American children leads to serious adverse conditions.

- *It depresses education outcomes for black students; as shown in this report, it lowers their standardized test scores.*
- *It widens performance gaps between white and black students.*
- *It reflects and bolsters segregation by economic status, with black students being more likely than white students to attend high-poverty schools.*
- *It means that the promise of integration and equal opportunities for all black students remains an ideal rather than a reality.*
- *In contrast, when black students have the opportunity to attend*

schools with lower concentrations of poverty and larger shares of white students they perform better, on average, on standardized tests.[lx]

African American children are still largely being relegated to separate and observably unequal schools, despite sweeping legislation and far more acceptance among the younger generations. The National Center for Education Statistics' National Assessment of Educational Progress (NAEP) performed the most comprehensive study of education performance in the country. Their findings on school segregation and student performance show that only about one in eight white students (12.9%) attend a school where the majority of students are African American, Hispanic, Asian, or American Indian. On the other hand, nearly seventy percent of African American children attend schools where students of color are the majority.

African American students are also in economically-segregated schools, meaning they are much more likely to be in impoverished communities. Only about a third of white students attend a high-poverty school, compared with over seventy percent of African American students.[lxi] The rise of Covid-19 made things worse. No doubt, the pandemic has been hard on the entire world but African American communities and their school-aged children have been adversely affected the most.

Proposals focused on school choice and expanding access to charter schools have been discussed, which is most often favored by centrist and Republican voters. What about Democrats' preferred solutions? This can be a complicated discussion because teachers' unions are largely allied with the Democratic party. However, what the teachers' unions want and advocate for is not necessarily the same as what Democrat-voting parents wish for their children. Ultimately, the vast majority of parents—Republicans or Democrats—want their children to receive a quality education in a safe environment that is conducive to learning.

The most frequently proposed solutions are early education programs like Head Start, with the hope that starting children in school earlier will improve learning outcomes. Taxpayer-funded community college is also a proposed solution frequently discussed, offering students an opportunity to shore up their math and reading skills prior to beginning university-level work. Funding these programs is a contentious issue, with both parties having their own views about how taxpayer dollars should be allocated.

As a voter and/or parent, it is important to ask your state officials and political candidates about their views on education and school choice.

CHAPTER 8
AMERICA'S INFRASTRUCTURE
★★★★★

"The core question about infrastructure is do we want to invest in ourselves as a nation and get more competitive or do we want to continue to muddle along and fall further behind?"
—Brendan Bechtel

The American Society of Civil Engineers (ASCE) produces an Infrastructure Report Card for the United States every four years, its most recent being in 2021. Our score? An unexceptional C- minus, which declares our overall infrastructure to be "mediocre, requires attention."[lxii] According to the Merriam-Webster dictionary, the term *infrastructure* means *"the system of public works of a country, state, or region."* Infrastructure includes public and private physical structures, systems and services such as, but is not necessarily limited to, the following:

- Aviation
- Bridges
- Broadband
- Dams
- Drinking water
- Energy
- Hazardous Waste
- Inland waterways

- Levees
- Public parks
- Ports
- Rail
- Roads
- Schools
- Solid waste
- Storm water
- Transit
- Wastewater

Basically, infrastructure includes everything that allows our country to function and makes our communities livable. You may not have thought about infrastructure in that context before, but you can probably appreciate the importance of each of the listed categories. And yet, we still often take our infrastructure for granted. Ask yourself, how much time do we spend thinking about infrastructure and how vital it is to our communities? More importantly, how much of our legislators' time and attention is focused on our infrastructure needs?

Each category listed above truly warrants its own discussion, but we will not discuss them all here. Besides, I doubt you have an interest in reading about them all. Instead, this writing will focus on three areas of particular concern: (i) public education, which we have already discussed in Chapter 7; (ii) roads and bridges; and (iii) trains and transit.

Roads and Bridges

In the most recent ASCE Report Card, our roads were given a D grade (poor, at risk) and our bridges were given a C (mediocre, requires attention). No matter where you live, but particularly if you live in any major city, it is unlikely that those grades are a surprise to you. Despite their importance, our roads are often left to crumble, with mere patchwork solutions being deployed as the only regular maintenance to fill potholes. In some cities, they do not even get that luxury. This is partly due to the complexities of determining who bears responsibility for paying any associated costs.

Have you ever driven on a road the day after it snows? The road you were on may have been thoroughly plowed, but then you cross an intersection, and that section of the road hasn't received the same level of care. Why is that? More likely than not, you entered a different municipality or town and the party responsible for paying for the plow and salt has changed.

Road maintenance is the same way. Some roads are maintained by the state, others by the city, and still others have sub-districts responsible for certain aspects of maintenance. The state may cover road construction, but the city manages potholes. The federal government is also responsible for certain roads, and of course interstate highways. With all these varying jurisdictions, it can be hard to know who to complain to about road conditions and who bears responsibility for maintaining them.

The political divide between Democrats and Republicans is usually not about whether to pass legislation that fund road construction or maintenance. Often, the disagreements are about all the other things that come with it. In political terms, it is called "pork."

When a bill is passed, it frequently includes provisions for things that may be unrelated to the primary purpose of the legislation. For instance, Congress recently passed President Biden's trillion-dollar "Infrastructure Bill" with most Republicans voting against it. Why would they oppose legislation supporting infrastructure? No doubt, both Republicans and Democrats want safe and well-maintained roads. Quite simply, Republicans opposed the legislation because most of the provisions in the bill had nothing to do with roads and bridges:

How much money does the bipartisan infrastructure bill spend on roads and bridges?

The Infrastructure Investment and Jobs Act, or BIF, totals $1.2 trillion in spending on traditional infrastructure, as well as broadband internet access and a number of green energy proposals.

Although this legacy media describes this bill as a boon for "roads and bridges," only approximately 10% of the bill — $110 billion — goes to roads and bridges. The White House says the $40 billion of that total designated specifically for bridges "is the single largest dedicated bridge investment since the construction of the interstate highway system" by the Eisenhower administration. The bill spends another $42 billion for airports and seaports, and $55 billion on fixing water pipes.[lxiii]

Republicans chafed at the amount of money going to green energy, which they decried as inefficient use of taxpayer dollars. They also protested the "congestion relief program" included in the bill, which encourages cities and municipalities to charge cars for traveling into city limits during peak hours, collect tolls from drivers, and hike the cost of parking in the city, which they argue essentially punishes people for driving their own cars.

To be clear, when Republicans are in power and pass their large omnibus bills, they do this too. It is just that the "pork" Republicans include in their bills is different from what Democrats prioritize. In short, Democrats and Republicans do not disagree on the need to build and maintain roads. Rather, they disagree over many of the non-core provisions included in the bill, and it is the American people who ultimately suffer because of the political wrangling.

Trains and Transit

The battle over trains and how much (if any) taxpayer money should be spent on them also ties into the conflict between Republicans and Democrats, and their views about the environment. Democrats often value and promote public transportation, including trains so fewer people have to drive. Large cities across the United States often have commuter train systems, and on the east coast some smaller cities do too. Though this is a common view generally espoused by the Democratic party, it is not necessarily one held by Democrats who reside in the country's interior.

In smaller towns in middle America, passenger rail transportation is less appealing. Train schedules can be uncertain, and trips can take a long time. Furthermore, the cost to build a new rail system may require the demolition or redirection of existing roadways. In middle America, there is not much appetite for that kind of change, regardless of party. So why do national politicians talk about building nationwide high-speed rail systems?

Often those conversations are driven by concerns about climate change and the environment, and are most often advocated by the Progressive wing of the Democrat party. They argue that mass transit reduces the level of carbon emissions released into the air. Therefore, they contend that, when feasible, mass transit should be used to mitigate risks to our planet. However, Republicans and Democrats outside of major metropolitan areas counter that building a train system potentially has adverse environmental effects that exceed the impact of driving cars.

There's also a question of trust and whether mass transit will be available when you need it most. Democrat and Republican voters share a healthy dose of skepticism toward the government and do not like the idea of having to rely on trains that may not work when you need them or may not run according to schedule. Access to a car provides a greater degree of freedom to travel whenever desired. This view has become even more pronounced in the wake of Covid-19 lockdowns.

Ultimately, trains are still important in terms of freight conveyance and tracks need to be maintained to keep supply lines moving. But their usefulness as a passenger conveyance (outside major metropolitan areas) appears to be largely a thing of the past, as only a third of Americans have stated they would use high-speed rail if it was available to them.[lxiv]

State vs. Federal Responsibility

Ultimately, the question of whether roads and other infrastructure funding should be handled by the state or federal government very often splits right down party lines, with Republicans favoring localism and the Democrats favoring top-down federal rule. As an example, if New Jersey residents believe that high-speed rail is a good use of their tax dollars, then generally, residents of Kansas will take no issue with it. However, Republicans may take issue when a federal bill is passed obligating residents of Kansas to pay higher taxes which will be used to fund expenses associated with building a high-speed rail system in New Jersey.

On the other hand, Democrats argue that permitting local governments to govern their own environmental regulations is akin to having a "smoking section" in a restaurant. From their perspective, we all breathe the same air, so pollution in Kansas can affect people in New Jersey. Therefore, they contend that laws addressing environmental concerns should be driven by federal mandate.

The question of local versus federal legislation and funding often leads to intense debate, and debates about infrastructure are no different. That should come as a shock to none of us as different states and regions have different priorities. As a voter, it is important to understand the distinction between federal and state powers and priorities, and how your elected officials view infrastructure projects and funding.

CHAPTER 9
ENERGY

*"American energy independence is an economic issue, an environmental
issue and a national security issue. It lowers gas prices,
creates American jobs, helps save our environment and lessens our
dependence on foreign oil."*
—Andy Warren

As of March 2022, debates centered on America's energy policy have become part of everyday discussions among mainstream Americans in a way not seen since the 1970s. The discussions about energy for the average American are usually focused on gas prices. Gas prices are an everyday concern for working Americans and a good reflection of whether our existing policies are effective.

At the time of this writing, the national average price for a gallon of gas is $4.26, whereas a year ago, it was $2.88. What could cause such a dramatic increase in only one year? In late February 2022, Russia, a major supplier of oil, invaded Ukraine, a sovereign nation and U.S. ally. In response, the U.S. and other countries embargoed Russian exports, including oil and gas. As a result, basic economic theory dictates that declining oil supplies will lead to increased prices in the absence of a corresponding decline in demand.

Interestingly, when President Biden took office, he pledged to end U.S. reliance on fossil fuels. "I guarantee you," Biden told New Hampshire voters on Sept. 16, 2019, "we're going to end fossil fuels."

The President's comments highlight a critical area of distinction between Democrats and Republicans. Debates between the two parties regarding America's energy policy are largely centered on their views about carbon emissions and the utilization of traditional versus alternative forms of energy to satisfy American energy needs. Meanwhile, as the two parties haggle over energy policy, the average American consumer is paying a heavy price at the pump.

Climate Change Legislation and Outcomes

Addressing climate change and trying to reverse its effects through carbon reduction is a pillar of the Democratic party platform. Following through on his campaign promises, President Biden made sweeping reforms during his first few months in office that fundamentally altered U.S. energy acquisition strategies:

- January 20, 2021: On the day of his inauguration, he signed an executive order that discontinued the Keystone XL Pipeline, which was designed to bring tar sands from Canada to American refineries.
- January 27, 2021: The Interior Department was directed to discontinue issuing oil and natural-gas leases on federal lands and in public waters.
- April 22, 2021: President Biden unveiled a "Climate Finance Plan" to "promote the flow" of capital "away from high-carbon investments."
- June 1, 2021: President Biden halted oil and gas leases in Alaska's Arctic National Wildlife Refuge.
- July 11, 2021: Treasury Secretary Janet Yellen said she expects multilateral development banks to "discourage new investments in fossil fuel-based power generation except where other options are not possible."

- August 16, 2021: Reuters reported, "Treasury to oppose development bank financing for most fossil fuel projects."
- December 10, 2021: Biden directed federal agencies to cease funding new, international, carbon-intensive fossil-fuel initiatives.
- January 31, 2022: The Biden administration raised the royalty rate that drilling companies must pay on oil and gas leases.
- February 24, 2022: Russia invaded Ukraine.
- February 28, 2022: The Biden Administration announced it would accept a federal court's rejection of its drilling-lease sales.[lxv]

Gasoline prices climbed 48.3% between President Biden's inauguration in January 2021 and Russia's invasion of Ukraine in February 2022, largely due to our need to import oil from foreign countries to replace our reduced domestic capacity and production. All of this may be somewhat confusing. After all, the Democratic platform emphasizes reducing fossil fuel consumption, right? So why are we importing it from foreign countries (especially countries that are hostile to American interests)? The reason is quite simple—politics!

Democratic leaders are doing exactly what they promised their constituents. They are (i) reducing American *production* of oil and gas products, and (ii) investing in alternative energy sources. However, Americans have not reduced their *use* of oil and gas. Green energy such as wind farms and solar energy are not at a level where they can replace fossil fuels on a large scale. This will take time and funding, for which Democratic leaders strongly advocate. In the meantime, while new energy technologies are being developed, Americans still need to put gas in their cars and power their homes. At this juncture, fossil fuels are the only existing, reliable way to do that at scale.

The desire for Americans to address climate and environmental concerns should certainly be taken seriously. However, current geopolitical issues and conflicts, rising energy prices and the fight for basic resources and necessities makes rising global temperatures seem like a problem that some argue is decades away and can be solved at some point in the future.

For many working-class Americans, the more immediate issue on their minds is how to keep gas in their cars and food on the table. This is the essence of the conflict between Democrats and Republicans when it comes to climate change legislation. Should our energy policy and legislation be focused on current needs, or those of the future? It truly requires a balancing act...and *that* is the challenge our legislators face when seeking to address America's energy needs.

Oil & OPEC

The Organization of the Petroleum Exporting Countries (OPEC) is an intergovernmental organization that creates a unified framework of global petroleum policies, including setting the price per barrel of petroleum. The price we pay at the pump is largely influenced by OPEC and its member nations:

- Algeria
- Angola
- Congo
- Equatorial Guinea
- Gabon
- Iran
- Iraq
- Kuwait
- Libya

- Nigeria
- Saudi Arabia
- United Arab Emirates
- Venezuela[lxvi]

You will notice two countries that are visibly not on this list. The United States produces and consumes roughly 20% of world oil production. However, the U.S. has not been a significant exporter of oil. Therefore, it makes sense that the U.S. would not be an OPEC affiliate. But what about Russia? They produce 11% of the world's oil production but only consume about 4%. Thus, Russia has been a net exporter of oil. So, why is Russia not a member of OPEC?

Like the U.S., other countries have their own political interests and motivations. If you will recall, gas prices were extremely low in 2020. Prices had not been that low since the late 1990s and early 2000s. But why? In simple terms, Saudi Arabia, a founding member of OPEC and the most influential nation in the coalition, intentionally flooded the market with oil because Russia failed to comply with one of OPEC's edicts.[lxvii] The increased supply had the intended effect of driving market prices lower. As an oil exporter, lower prices negatively impacted the amount of revenue Russia could generate from the sale of oil to other countries. Prior to 2020, Russia was a non-OPEC cooperating provider and may well have been invited to join, but it was not on good terms with Saudi Arabia. The U.S. reaped the benefits of that price war, though most Americans probably weren't driving as much during the pandemic.

In 2020, low U.S. gas prices were also supported by the fact that, at the time, the U.S. was no longer a net importer of oil. However, U.S. production has since declined due to current government policies, as noted earlier. As a result, the U.S. has once again become a net importer of oil. Therefore, absent a change in policy, our ability to access petroleum products and the prices we pay will continue to be largely influenced by OPEC and its member states.

Fracking

Fracking has been a hot-button issue over the years, mostly due to environmental concerns. Many Americans, however, are not entirely sure what fracking involves.

> *Fracking is the process of drilling into the earth and directing a high-pressure mixture of water, sand and chemicals at a rock layer in order to release the gas inside. The wells can be drilled vertically or horizontally in order to release the gas. The term fracking refers to how the rock is fractured apart by the high-pressure mixture.*[lxviii]

Though fracking has generally been considered a vital part of the U.S. strategy to achieve energy independence, the process has been the subject of much debate among environmentalists for some time, with their major concerns revolving around an increase in earthquakes in areas where fracking occurred, along with potential drinking water contamination and a more common occurrence of sink holes. Environmentalists are also concerned that fracking will distract lawmakers and energy firms from investing in green and renewable energy sources.

In 2015, the Brookings Institute devoted an entire article extolling the virtues of fracking, including lower energy costs, more reliable energy sources, and overall improvement in quality of life for the average consumer, though they also noted the environmental concerns.[lxix] Although the economic benefits are unassailable, and the U.S. Geological Survey has gone on record saying that the increase in earthquakes in the Midwest is *not* directly caused by hydraulic fracking,[lxx] a fair amount of voters, regardless of party affiliation, continue to view fracking with a degree of caution.

Continental Pipelines

In the United States, there are presently thirty oil and gas pipelines in existence. However, as noted earlier, the highly contested Keystone XL Pipeline has been halted and is not currently in use. Though the Keystone XL Pipeline was perhaps the most well-known, it is far from the only continental pipeline designed to transport oil, tar sands, and natural gas throughout the country. These pipelines are mostly underground and serve to transport crude oil from onshore and offshore oil fields to refineries, and to transport natural gas.

In general, pipelines do not present the types of concerns associated with fracking, although they are still a target of environmentalists. They are generally viewed as safe and have not been shown to increase risk of pollution or any other material concerns (except possibly injury to personnel during construction). Pipelines are a vital part of the United States' domestic energy policy and the primary mechanism through which we are able to transport oil and gas from repositories to the consumer.

Domestic production of traditional energy sources such as oil and gas, as well as the utilization of pipelines, is most often opposed by Democrats. However, there are differences in perspectives even amongst Democrats regarding domestic oil production and the utilization of pipelines that transport the oil. In Pennsylvania, for instance, Democrats in the State House of Representatives called on President Biden to restart construction on the Keystone XL pipeline, citing soaring gas prices for their constituents and general concern over reliance on foreign oil.

Although Pennsylvania has many municipalities that consistently vote for Republican candidates, its state-wide and federal elections often lean towards Democratic candidates. Thus, the divergent views on energy production and pipelines is noteworthy because constituent views on the issue are not always driven by party politics but rather the practical realities of voters. While some political issues can easily be viewed through the prism of left versus right, energy production and the utilization of pipelines appears to be viewed in more practical terms.

Results-Based Solutions

A good question to ask an incumbent or a candidate for national office would be how they plan to maintain affordable energy for Americans. Depending on the individual, their party affiliation and the state in which they are running, the answers may vary wildly. Some will focus on making renewable energy sources less expensive. Some will focus on increasing production of fossil fuels. These both have their benefits and drawbacks, as we have previously discussed. It will be for you, the voter, to decide which method you believe is most advantageous and which is best for your family and future.

Another potential energy source is nuclear power. However, unlike other nations, Americans have not yet advocated for nuclear power in a meaningful way. Even though about 20% of U.S. energy is derived from nuclear energy,[lxxi] most policymakers are hesitant to advocate for devoting more resources to maintaining the nuclear power plants we have or increasing their utilization to make nuclear power a primary source of energy in the U.S. Understandably, the American public has been hesitant to consider nuclear power as a long-term solution for our energy needs, despite the fact it is considered a clean, reliable energy source far superior to fossil fuels. Catastrophes like Fukushima and Three-Mile Island loom large in the American mind, as well as internationally publicized nuclear meltdowns such as the weapons-grade nuclear facility, Chernobyl.

Despite the fear generated from these isolated incidents, it may well be that nuclear power can offer a suitable energy source that is clean enough for environmentally-conscious Democrats while also being reliable and inexpensive enough for cost-conscious Republicans. Ultimately, you must decide which sources of energy and energy policies are best for our country and which candidate you believe will be most effective advocating on your behalf. Though it may not always be top of mind at the ballot box, energy policy is often a major factor that not only impacts national security, but also impacts our cost of living and ability to maintain the lifestyle we currently enjoy.

CHAPTER 10

DEFENSE

"There is nothing so likely to produce peace as to be well prepared to meet an enemy."
— President George Washington

The United States was born out of conflict, so it makes sense that for much of our history, an enormous amount of our national budget has been devoted to defense. Having recently concluded a twenty-year military conflict in Iraq and Afghanistan, most Americans have developed very strong opinions about the U.S. military, its role in our society, and how our government leaders wield our military might.

Following President Biden's inauguration in 2021, questions about the role of our military and America's role in foreign affairs became the focus of intense debate. A 2021 survey administered by the Ronald Reagan Institute and involving more than 2,500 participants highlights important findings.

The study found that trust in the U.S. military has apparently eroded significantly in recent years. However, the armed forces in general remain a respected institution. According to the survey, only about fifty-six percent of respondents said they have "a great deal of trust and confidence" in the military, which is a decrease from seventy percent in 2018.

About sixty-one percent of survey participants supported maintaining current U.S. troops levels overseas. In addition, roughly sixty-one percent of participants also said they believe that internal threats are a greater or equal challenge for America than external threats. It is possible that the survey results could have been skewed by the political turmoil that followed the 2020 election and the fact that the survey was conducted shortly after the January 6, 2021 riots in Washington D.C. Admittedly, the survey reflects only a small sample of American citizens and may not be representative of the broader U.S. population. Nonetheless, the survey results do provide some insight into the American psyche. What is clear is that societal views about our military and its role in the world is evolving.

"There has been a rising concern over domestic division and political violence in the United States and for a number of years now… We see in this poll that Americans are experiencing a sense of pessimism in almost every question [regarding] confidence or trust or reliance on allies. The numbers are generally ticking down."[lxxii]

Overall, it seems Americans have a high regard for our military history and the wars fought by previous generations, while being somewhat skeptical of more recent military conflicts.

The Purpose and History of the U.S. Military

The first iteration of the U.S. military was the Continental Army, formed in 1775 to fight the American Revolution under the command of George Washington. The need for an Army was unquestioned at that time as Americans fought for independence from the British. However, after the Treaty of Paris in 1783 (which officially ended the American Revolutionary War) and the recognition of the United States as a sovereign nation, some began to question whether there was still a need for a standing Army. Nonetheless, the War Office (later called the War Department) was formed in 1790 and continued to oversee the defense of our newly created country.

The Mexican-American War (1846-1848) led to the creation of a more formalized fighting force that included both a standing Army, as well as conscripts, who were compulsory enlisted into the military but were required to wear a uniform only during wartime. This model continued during the Civil War, as Americans fought one another in the struggle to end slavery and reverse the course of history for those states that had seceded from the Union.

The War and Navy Departments continued to evolve (as separate organizations, reporting separately to the president) for the next several years with more conflicts, including the first World War. To remove existing silos and create a more cohesive defense strategy, Congress created the U.S. Department of Defense in 1947 after the U.S. entered World War II. The Department of Defense was comprised of the Departments of the Navy, Army, and Air Force. The U.S. Marines fall under the Department of the Navy. Today, the Department of Defense is headquartered at the Pentagon and is headed by the Joint Chiefs of Staff (Generals from the Army, Navy, Air Force, and Marines). From its inception, the Department of Defense was designed to provide military might to enforce the national policy of the United States. Yet, "[t]he original National Security Act of 1947 provided the Secretary of Defense with limited authority and staff to exercise control. However, subsequent amendments to the Act in 1949, 1953, and 1958 strengthened the authority and ability of the Secretary to direct defense policy. With the 1949 amendment, the modern Department of Defense was established"[lxxiii]

After the Vietnam War, and the ensuing backlash against the heavy loss of American lives, the Department of Defense transitioned to an all-volunteer military force in 1973. As a result, there can be no compulsory military draft without an official act of Congress. To be clear, males are still required to register with Selective Service when they turn eighteen years of age because Congress could, in theory, reinstate the draft in the event of a national emergency.

African American Contributions to Military History

African Americans have fought in every U.S. conflict, from the Revolutionary War to the Iraq-Afghanistan conflict, though many of their contributions have only recently come to light and gained the recognition they so richly deserve. Henry Johnson, for instance, a member of the "Harlem Hellfighters" distinguished himself during WWI by single-handedly fighting off twenty Germans to save a fellow soldier from capture—all while injured and armed with only a knife.[lxxiv]

The military has provided a path for upward mobility for many, including African Americans, but that path has far too often been paved with injustice and racism toward these men and women who fought (and died) for our country. The Tuskegee Airmen, for instance, were the first Black military aviators in the U.S. Army Air Corps (AAC), which would eventually become the U.S. Air Force. These groundbreaking aviators were trained at the Tuskegee Army Airfield in Alabama and would go on to fly more than 15,000 individual sorties in Europe and North Africa during World War II. Those soldiers earned more than 150 Distinguished Flying Crosses and stood as a rebuke to the existing segregation in the Armed Forces. Despite prevailing racist attitudes, the Tuskegee Airmen showed the world that African Americans could (and did) learn to fly and operate sophisticated aircraft.[lxxv]

Despite their contributions and obvious skill, it took some time for the complicated history of racism to be rectified within the Armed Forces. For instance, General Douglas MacArthur was famous for his acts of bravery and brilliant tactics during World War II. Unfortunately, he made it clear he did not approve of having African American regiments assigned to him and kept them away from the fighting as much as possible, deeming them inferior to white soldiers. He did this even as African Americans on land, sea, and air distinguished themselves in battle.

Unfortunately, MacArthur's opinion was common throughout

most of American history, with World War II serving as the watershed period that solidified the acceptance of African Americans into all American armed forces. For instance, at the start of World War II, the Marine Corps had a simple policy governing African Americans: it did not and would not accept them! In fact, in April 1941, the Commandant of the Marine Corps, Major General Thomas Holcomb, declared that African Americans had no place in the organization he led. "If it were a question of having a Marine Corps of 5,000 whites or 250,000 Negroes," he said, "I would rather have the whites."[lxxvi]

The Navy, at that time, generally allowed admittance of African Americans, but only in small numbers, and only as cooks. However, after President Franklin Roosevelt won his third term, he understood that the African American vote had been instrumental to his re-election campaign and he took measures to improve acceptance and treatment of African Americans in the military.

The Navy, Marines, and Coast Guard dragged their feet at the mandate, and it took three full years before they finally announced that African Americans would be admitted into general service. It should be noted that the Army had been enlisting African Americans since the Civil War, although they served in segregated units until 1948, when President Truman abolished segregation in the Armed Forces.[lxxvii]

Despite the fact that African Americans had served in the military since the days of the Revolutionary War, it was not until 1940 that an African American finally achieved the rank of Brigadier General. That ground-breaking distinction goes to Benjamin O. Davis who faithfully served our country during a career that spanned forty years of military service and two world wars. Since that time, African Americans have continued to distinguish themselves at all levels of military service. General Colin Powell, who passed away in 2021, served as this nation's first African American Secretary of Defense after a distinguished career in the armed forces, including serving on the Joint Chiefs of Staff. On

August 6, 2022, General Michael Langley made history when he was appointed the first African American Four-Star General of the Marine Corps. The achievements of these leaders and other soldiers who selflessly serve and sacrifice on behalf of our nation should inspire us all.

It is noteworthy, however, that African Americans comprise only 12.4 percent of the U.S. population but account for roughly twenty percent of the armed forces. And yet, the number of African Americans who have attained the ranks of General or Admiral remains lower than their representative numbers would indicate.[lxxviii] Thus, while there has certainly been progress, there remains work to be done to erase the effects of past policies.

The Role of Defense in Foreign Policy

Most Americans understand that past military conflicts have, in many respects, been required to preserve our freedom and our way of life. You will find very few, if any, Americans who believe it was a mistake for the U.S. to enter either of the World Wars and most Americans believe that the Revolutionary War was just and a good decision. However, opinions vary widely regarding U.S. engagement in military conflicts occurring since the 1950s.

The Vietnam War provided American civilians with the first near-real-time video footage of the carnage and destruction of combat on the battlefield. Since that time, Americans have been markedly less enthusiastic about going to war than previous generations. Technically, the U.S. *has not* officially gone to war since World War II. Rather, we have engaged in military conflicts, ordered by the president but not voted on by Congress. This means that America has engaged in military conflicts without the support of the American people. In those instances, whether "war" or "military conflicts," it is always prudent to have the support of the American public if we are risking American lives and using taxpayer resources.

In addition, Americans have very different views about the circumstances under which the United States should enter armed conflict. There have been a series of armed conflicts where Americans have been deployed to "protect human life," such as Somalia and Kosovo. Many believe this is a laudable reason, but it is hardly a view that is uniformly accepted by the American public. The military, at the direction of the president, may intervene in a perceived genocide on some occasions, but not others, even if there is a much greater loss of human life (e.g., Rwanda). The perceived inconsistencies often lead to confusion or even frustration amongst the American public.

The question for the president and legislators to consider is: Is this issue worth American blood and treasure? Engaging in armed conflict, even if it seems one-sided, such as the first Iraq War, still carries risk and our leaders must evaluate the consequences of intervention, as well as the consequences of inaction. The American people will form their own opinions, perhaps using those opinions to inform their voting decisions when they go to the ballot box. The second Iraq War, for instance, was highly contentious, with roughly half of America opposing it. President George W. Bush still won reelection, but the results were closer than they likely would have been otherwise, especially considering the wave of patriotism that immediately followed the 9/11 attacks.

When making foreign policy decisions and managing foreign relations, the U.S. must always weigh the possibility of using an armed response. President Obama was famously excoriated after he said if Syria used chemical weapons, it constituted a "red line" that would trigger an armed response from the U.S. However, when credible evidence surfaced that Bashar al Assad had used chemical weapons, President Obama decided not to deploy an armed response.

However, President Trump was likewise excoriated for choosing to retaliate against Syria for the same reason—chemical weapons. In one case, inaction led to criticism. In the other, action led to public anger.[lxxix] Both made a political calculation based on the circumstances at the time and both were heavily criticized. For this reason, many argue that perhaps it would be better if we returned those powers to the exclusive jurisdiction of Congress. From their perspective, doing so would ensure that most Americans are supportive of military engagement before we commit our troops and resources. Further, it would limit the power of the president to unilaterally commit the U.S. to armed conflict.

Other Countries' Reliance on U.S. Military

In the post-World War II era, it has been widely accepted that the U.S., in many respects, has become the world's policeman. When young, idealistic Americans look at France and other European Union member states, they often wonder why the U.S. can't have such generous social safety nets. Why do European countries spend so much money on their citizens while we spend a substantial amount of our federal budget on defense? The reason for that is simple: our allies, NATO countries specifically, do not spend as much on their militaries because they have the security of knowing that if conflicts arise, the U.S. military—the greatest fighting force in the world—will come to their defense. This reliance on U.S. armed forces is, in part, what makes our country so influential. Ironically, it is also a major reason why the U.S. is often resented.

Indeed, Europeans cooperated with the U.S. program because it created conditions under which both the United States and Europe flourished. The United States assisted Europe's postwar economic recovery with 13 billion dollars of aid in the form of the Marshall Plan. (In today's dollars, roughly 113 billion.) It midwifed the groupings and treaties that would become the European Union. It brought Europe under the U.S. security umbrella with the NATO treaty. Article V of the treaty, its most important element, declares that an attack on one member of

NATO is an attack on all members. These policies were intended not only to counter the Soviet Union, but to condition Europe's prosperity upon its integration into a single market, with free movement of goods, capital and labor. The founders of these institutions fully intended them to be the foundations of a United States of Europe, much like the United States of America. Profound economic interdependence, they believed, would make further European wars impossible.[xxx]

However, many Americans now wish to stay out of conflicts that do not directly involve the U.S. As a result, European nations have started looking to be more self-sufficient, even pitching the idea of an EU Army. That idea, however, has not yet materialized.

Sole Superpower?

After the fall of the Soviet Union, the U.S. found itself as the world's sole major military power. No other country could conceivably compete in open warfare. However, the face of war has changed along with technology. The 9/11 attacks taught us that threats will not necessarily come from nation-states. A country can find itself under attack from loose webs of terrorist organizations, leaving a standing Army with no clear target to attack in retaliation. In addition, many state actors have shifted their attacks to the cyber world, keeping their actions covert and making it difficult to identify the origins of the threat.

Finally, when it comes to military strength, some argue that China is emerging as a real threat to America's sole superpower status as it has made bold moves in defiance of U.S. interests, including aggressive incursions into the South China sea, anti-democracy crackdowns in Hong Kong, and openly threatening Taiwan's sovereignty.

Seething at what they consider humiliations inflicted by Western powers—from the Opium War to what the Chinese call "unequal" treaties that sapped their sovereignty—China is on a mission to regain the upper hand. As Xi put it, the country "will never again tolerate being bullied by any nation." That's the goal behind much of his current policies, from a significant buildup of military capabilities to state-funded programs aimed at helping China overtake the West in technology. More and more, China's diplomacy turns threatening when faced with challenges from other countries, whether the U.S., India, or Australia.

What becomes clear from an examination of China's history is that the Chinese don't just want to be a great power—they believe they deserve to be. In centuries past, the Chinese thought their sovereign had a right to rule "all under Heaven." Due to the realities of technology and distance, China's reach usually remained regional. But now, in the age of globalization, Beijing's influence may achieve that lofty goal.[lxxxi]

Americans will likely continue to explore the role of our military, the level of spending on defense, and our responsibly to defend not only our own borders, but also those of our allies. In addition, debates will surely continue about whether the U.S. should serve as the world's military superpower and *de facto* world police. These are serious questions that voters must ask of themselves and their elected officials. For example, are you concerned that China or some other country could have the level of global influence that the U.S. has enjoyed for so long? As of now, China appears to be the only plausible alternative that could potentially challenge America's standing on the global stage. But empires inevitably rise and fall. Therefore, when making voting decisions about the military, more than perhaps any other issue, the future must be considered as you decide which political candidates can provide the leadership our country so desperately needs.

CHAPTER 11

IMMIGRATION

"I had always hoped that this land might become a safe and agreeable asylum to the virtuous and persecuted part of mankind, to whatever nation they might belong."
—President George Washington

L
ike many issues in politics, "immigration" has become a hot-button issue, one that many regular voters do not feel comfortable discussing in social settings. There are many reasons for Americans' hesitance to openly discuss immigration at all. Or if they do, it is only to offer a generic response similar to what you might find on a bumper sticker: "Diversity is our strength" or "America is a nation of immigrants."

Such responses are certainly true. After all, with the exception of Native Americans, we are all descendants of those who came to America from another place (some willingly, others not). Each American has an interest in the immigration agenda of our elected officials and how immigrants are vetted before being granted the privilege of residing or working in the United States. And it is a privilege, not a right! It is also prudent to police illegal immigration, as an unsecured border would permit anyone to enter our country, with no way for us to discern their motives.

These do not seem like controversial statements and yet, in recent years, they have been. Many accusations of racism against non-white immigrants or xenophobia get casually tossed around when discussing the most basic tenets of immigration policy. And, if we are to be honest, part of the reason these accusations seem to gain traction is because many Americans are aware of our country's history of intentionally excluding non-white immigrants.

Early U.S. Immigration Policy

The 1790 Naturalization Act was designed expressly to prohibit non-white people from becoming American citizens. The Act specifically required that any applicant for U.S. citizenship be a "free white person." Of course, this excluded white people (often Irish) who were indentured servants as well... but only temporarily. The Act also required two years of residence in the country and being of "good moral character."[lxxxii] This meant an Irish indentured servant, once free of his contract, could start his two-year residency requirement and then be applicable for citizenship. African Americans and other people of color, based on the Act's requirements, would never be eligible.

It is hard to align the express discrimination of the 1790 Naturalization Act with the idea that "all men are created equal." Yet, in 1795, Congress passed another Naturalization Act that made it even more onerous to become a citizen, extending the residency requirement from two years to five years. Then in 1798, it was further extended to fourteen years.

The right of U.S. citizenship was not granted to those of African origin until 1870, five years after the end of the Civil War and the assassination of President Abraham Lincoln.

These expressly exclusionary policies were not limited to African Americans. They also applied to Asians and southern Europeans, including Italians, Spaniards, and Greeks, who at that time were not considered white.

As a matter of fact, in 1921 and 1924, Congress passed laws expressly designed to limit immigration from southern Europe, capping total annual immigration and imposing quotas based on immigrant nationality that favored northern and western European countries. It was not until 1952, when Congress passed the Immigration and Nationality Act (also called The McCarran-Walter Act), that race was removed as an explicit basis for excluding an immigrant from becoming a naturalized U.S. citizen. However, a national-origins quota remained.[lxxxiii]

The Civil Rights Era and the Effect on Immigration

For the United States, 1965 was a pivotal year for legislation that addressed racial justice and equality among citizens. It also marked the year of the landmark Immigration and Nationality Act that overhauled the immigration system as a whole, focusing on skilled immigrants and family reunification, rather than quotas from specific countries.[lxxxiv] The law also limited, for the first time, the migration of citizens from other countries in the Western Hemisphere. Prior to this Act, people from Central America had been allowed to enter the U.S. without many restrictions. The enactment of the 1965 Immigration and Nationality Act, has largely resulted in the migration of people, both legal and illegal, from Asia and Latin America, rather than Europe.

Refugees, Asylum, and DACA

The change in immigration patterns and demographics coalesced with a shift in American sentiment that some parts of the world are dangerous, often suffering from war or targeted persecution of minorities. In these cases, many Americans believe it is the duty of the United States to accept refugees from those war-torn nations, regardless of whether the refugees have skills beneficial to the U.S. job market. In light of this sentiment, in 1990, lawmakers created the "temporary protective status" that shielded immigrants, mainly Central Americans, from deportation to countries facing natural disasters, armed conflicts, or other extraordinary conditions.[lxxxv]

In 1986, Congress enacted the Immigration Reform and Control Act, which provided legal clemency to millions of illegal immigrants, mainly from Latin America, as long as they had entered the U.S. before 1982. However, the law was designed to be a last call of sorts and also imposed sanctions on employers who thereafter hired illegal immigrants. But, voters on both sides of the political divide would quickly remind us that the legislation did not prevent undocumented workers from finding employment in the U.S. Nor was it the end of voters' concerns about immigration.

Democrat and Democrat-leaning voters tend to focus on the need to protect unauthorized workers from being abused, underpaid, or otherwise exploited, as well as typically advocating for a pathway to citizenship, regardless of the legality of their entry into the U.S.

Republican and Republican-leaning voters, on the other hand, tend to support immigration accomplished through legal means (including authorized refugees) and they are most concerned with border security and protecting the wages of American laborers, low-skilled workers, and other members of the working class.

The most recent change in immigration policy, and perhaps the most contentious, is the 2012 Deferred Action for Childhood Arrivals (DACA) program. DACA is the product of an Executive Order that allowed young adults who had been brought to the country illegally to apply for deportation relief and a work permit. In 2014, DACA was expanded to offer similar benefits to some unauthorized-immigrant parents of U.S.-born children. However, DACA was not fully implemented as twenty-six states instituted legal proceedings challenging its constitutionality.

The Left/Right Divide

Executive Orders, much like Supreme Court rulings, do not reflect the majority opinion in the U.S. Having a new law passed by Congress typically means that there is a will among the majority of Americans for action to be taken. Of course, no law has universal support, but Congress passing laws means the representatives reasonably believe they will not be voted out of office by their constituents for helping pass the law. For executive orders, on the other hand, the president who orders them is primarily concerned with the opinion of his base, which often means they have less support from the general public. Furthermore, executive orders can be revoked as soon as the president leaves office, creating instability.

Both Democratic and Republican party views on immigration are as nuanced as the history of immigration itself. However, the arguments made by either side have surprisingly remained relatively consistent since the 1980s. Although their core beliefs may differ, Republicans and Democrats both support legal immigration, as revealed by Pew Research. However, the number of immigrants which is acceptable and the countries from which they are permitted remains a point of contention, as well as how best to respond to sudden influxes of refugees. But the most divisive issues are centered on what should be done about illegal immigration, the people who are caught breaking immigration law, as well as the U.S. businesses that incentivize and facilitate the law-breaking.

What the Right Says

Republicans and Republican-leaning independents often focus on two issues: (i) equal application of the law and (ii) the security of the U.S. (and its citizens). While critics of the Republican view often allege that they are "anti-immigration," that is an oversimplification. For instance, the main Republican opposition to the DACA executive order was that the immigration laws that required the prosecution and deportation of illegal immigrants, even those brought here as children are still laws. In the commission of DACA, no existing federal laws were repealed and no new ones were passed. In short, they argued that the practical effect of the executive order was that existing laws didn't apply to a certain group of people. Republican opposition was centered on grounds that these actions were not consistent with past precedent and exceeded presidential authority.

In 1996—which for some, may seem like ages ago—Roy Beck laid out the case against facilitating immigration, both legal and illegal, in the Washington Post. His points of contention remain applicable to modern opponents of immigration and, if anything, have become even more pressing:

> *Until recently, policymakers and politicians of every stripe had ignored what public opinion polls found to be the public's growing dissatisfaction with the abnormally high level of immigration. Majority public opinion can be shallow, fleeting, and wrong, but an honest look at major trends during the recent mass immigration shows that ordinary Americans' concerns can hardly be dismissed as narrow and unenlightened:*
>
> - *Whole industries in the 1970s and 1980s reorganized to exploit compliant foreign labor, with the result that conditions have deteriorated for all workers in those industries.*
> - *Long trends of rising U.S. wages have been reversed.*
> - *Poverty has increased.*
> - *The middle-class way of life has come under siege; income disparities have widened disturbingly.*
> - *Aggressive civil rights programs to benefit the descendants of slavery have been watered down, co-opted, and undermined because of the unanticipated volume of new immigration. A nearly half-century march of economic progress for black Americans has been halted and turned back.*
> - *The culture—and even language—of many local communities*

has been transformed against the wishes of their native inhabitants. Instead of spawning healthy diversity, immigration has turned many cities into caldrons of increased ethnic tension and divisiveness.

- A stabilizing U.S. population with low birth rates (like other advanced nations) has become the most rapidly congesting industrialized nation in the world (resembling trends in Third World countries). Vast tracts of remaining farmland, natural habitat, and ecosystems have been destroyed to accommodate the growing population. Environmental progress has been set back by the addition of tens of millions of new polluters.

- Numerous organized crime syndicates headquartered in the new immigrants' home countries have gained solid beachheads of operations. Law enforcement agencies have been confounded just as they thought they were near victory over the crime organizations that other ethnic groups had brought with them during the Great Wave.

The task before the nation in setting a fair level of immigration is not about race or some vision of a homogeneous white America; it is about protecting and enhancing the United States' unique experiment in democracy for all Americans, including recent immigrants, regardless of their particular ethnicity. It is time to confront the true costs and benefits of immigration numbers, which have skyrocketed beyond our society's ability to handle them successfully.[lxxxvi]

In 2021, Customs and Border Protection experienced a record-high number of encounters at the border, almost two million, in fact. With such massive numbers of foreign nationals coming into the country, often unvetted and unnoticed, many Americans, particularly those in border states, are beginning to get uneasy with the rates of illegal immigration that is going seemingly unchecked. It becomes even more concerning to them when considering European Union countries and how many of them have simply allowed massive waves of migrants into their country with no vetting. For example, many of the migrants accepted by European countries come from societies that are wildly different than (and some openly hostile to) liberal Western democracy. The problem is so severe in some communities (specifically in France and Britain), that it prompted the publication of *Strange Death of Europe* by Douglas Murray.

Some Americans who lean Republican, or perhaps have switched parties due to the immigration issue, are focused on security for their families and being assured that we are not allowing criminals to come into our country, putting communities at risk. The U.S., by virtue of its size, may not necessarily be in the same overwhelming situation as European countries. However, Right-leaning voters and many centrists have likely been influenced by the chaos on our southern border or otherwise heard about criminals who have been apprehended (many not even from Central America), and understandably have become concerned or even afraid for their safety.

What the Left Says

Democrats have advocated to change the phrase "illegal alien" to "undocumented worker," arguing that no person is illegal. They also emphasize that, with the exception of Native Americans, all Americans descended from immigrants. Thus, how can it be moral or acceptable for us to restrict or ban immigration?

In recent years, critics have argued that the U.S., through its past (and potentially current) foreign policy decisions, is partly responsible for the difficult living conditions of poor people in some countries, particularly Latin and South America. As the most powerful country in the world, they contend the U.S. has a responsibility to accommodate immigrants who want to relocate to the United States.

Prior generations held similar views, though only in terms of legal immigrants. It is only recently that more vocal members of the Democratic caucus have advocated for illegal immigrants to be treated equally. That view has led many Democrats to be described, fairly or unfairly, as being "against borders." To be clear, there is a fringe element that does not believe in sovereign nations, but they are a vanishingly small minority of the Democratic party. However, most Democrats do believe in generous and liberal allowance of immigrants in the U.S., as demonstrated by the Democratic National Committee's statement on their stance on Immigration:

> ...*Democrats will continue to work toward comprehensive immigration reform that fixes our nation's broken immigration system, improves border security, prioritizes enforcement so we are targeting criminals – not families, keeps families together, and strengthens our economy.* [emphasis added]

> *Democrats know the importance of our country's history as a nation of immigrants. We honor our fundamental values by treating all people who come to the United States with dignity and respect, and we always seek to embrace — not to attack — immigrants.*

The question then becomes, with illegal immigrants, how can Americans assure that it is, in fact, families who are coming into the U.S., and not criminals, including human traffickers?

As the party of reproductive freedom, Democrats often point to the dwindling birth rates of native U.S. citizens, thus requiring a steady influx of immigrants. The desire for more immigrants is not solely driven by the need for workers but also for consumers. Recall that the U.S. has a fiat currency and operates in a global financial system that is backed by debt.[lxxxvii] Thus, some economic theorists are concerned that if the population and consumption dwindles below a certain level, the entire financial system would be adversely impacted.

Some market observers believe that most western nations, including the U.S., have already dropped below an acceptable replacement rate. Some even argue that European nations like the U.K., France, and Germany have dropped so low that they are past the point of no return. They surmise that there is no amount of "family-making" that native-born English, French, and Germans can do now to maintain their population. It is headed off a cliff, they contend. They warn that the U.S. native population rate is not yet at that threshold, but it is trending in that direction. Democrats, who ardently advocate for personal choice, would never suggest Americans have more babies. They more logically say that since Americans have chosen not to have children at acceptable replacement rates, then we must simply import willing consumers from elsewhere. If nothing else, it is a pragmatic solution in their minds.

African Americans and Immigration

We have already spoken about the income disparities between white Americans and African Americans (as a group, not specific individuals) in that African Americans disproportionately make up the working and lower class. Additionally, on a per capita basis, African Americans are disproportionately represented among welfare participants. Like Roy Beck laid out in his opposition to immigration, programs like welfare are often perceived as being designed to assist the descendants of slavery in the U.S., reparations if you will. Thus, it makes sense that rising numbers of immigrants, both legal and not, would disproportionately affect African Americans. In a 2010 survey of African Americans on their opinions of immigration, there were some interesting findings:

- *The immigration debate as it is being played out on the national stage is not a high priority for the African American press in terms of its regular news coverage.*

- *The competition and conflict frame is not a dominant frame in the African American press' news coverage.*
- *African Americans are more supportive of immigrant rights than whites when it comes to issues of discrimination, unfairness, and injustice.*
- *African Americans are more fearful than whites of negative economic effects of immigration both on the country as a whole and on their own job opportunities.*
- *Longitudinal research suggests that African American public opinion is shifting in the direction of more negative attitudes and beliefs about immigration and immigrants.[lxxxviii]*

Since the majority of African Americans lean Democrat in their voting registration, it is perhaps not surprising that they are generally supportive of "immigrant rights," while at the same time being concerned about the financial repercussions of immigration.

Immigration is an important issue and the resulting trade-offs to employ an effective immigration system must be closely examined. Thus, it is incumbent on voters to challenge their candidates to understand their stance on immigration, especially during Primary races. Even if your values align best with the platform of a particular party, it is important to understand the differences in views of candidates within that party.

Looking to Other Countries for Solutions

Modern voters are often conflicted about how to handle immigration and thus may not know which candidate to support. Americans value their own culture and don't want a different one to overwhelm their community. But they also generally understand that the world can be a dangerous place. Few adults in the U.S. are ignorant of what happens in towns like Juarez, Mexico. We know the danger that innocent people experience while just trying to get to work and raise their families. And during times of crisis and hardship, Americans have shown a propensity to be empathetic and generous. Most Americans do not want to send families back to the danger and/or poverty they fled. So, what can be done to split the difference?

The British government recently came up with a novel way to handle their unsustainable influx of migrants. Of course, islands do not have land-based migrants walking over an unsecured border. Instead, migrants—primarily from North Africa and the Middle East—travel by boat from Calais, France to England, a journey that is dangerous and ruled over by ruthless criminal gangs who exploit the migrants (not unlike the so-called "coyotes" who traffic humans across our southern border).

Britain has announced a pilot plan to address its continuing refugee crisis with a view towards mitigating the risk of harm that could result by sending migrants back to their countries of origin. The U.K. interior ministry has signed a deal with Rwanda to send many migrants arriving in the U.K. to the East African nation where their asylum claims can be processed. Under the plan, migrants may be afforded an opportunity to permanently settle in Rwanda, as it is generally considered safe, has many work opportunities for migrants, and a diverse religious culture that will be more amenable to North African migrants than the very secular Britain.

The authorities in Britain insist this new partnership with Rwanda is designed to combat criminal gangs that exploit migrants. After 28,000 people crossed the English Channel from France in small boats last year and several drowned, efforts to halt those potentially deadly journeys have included cooperation with French police, payments to the French government and the threatened use of British naval ships to push *migrant boats back from the shores of southern England. None have worked, and so now U.K. authorities will pay around $150 million to the Rwandan government to accept single male travelers that they say have arrived in the U.K. illegally. The U.K.'s Interior Minister Priti Patel traveled to Rwanda to sign the agreement with her Rwandan counterparts.*

"We, as two ministers, stand here today, absolutely committed to changing some of the norms around the broken global migration system because, for too long, other countries and, by the way, naysayers just sit on their hands and have been watching people die.[lxxxix]

This is a very unusual move to be sure, but it is one that is necessitated by the fact that Britain is very, very small. Their housing is already scarce and inflated, and the sudden influx of immigrants has created a host of challenges.

The United States is a much bigger country and is not hampered by the same land and space constraints as faced in Britain. However, it may be beneficial for the U.S. to consider a relocation program where migrants can be strategically moved to different states or U.S. territories, ensuring the migrants' safety, but not overwhelming the local population of states on the Southern border.

Ultimately it depends on your own values. If you believe that borders are at best arbitrary and, at worst, harmful and exclusionary, then the progressive wing of the Democrat party would likely best serve your interests. If you are on the other extreme and disagree with all immigration, both legal and illegal, you will likely not find a mainstream candidate who will run on that platform. As we have discussed, simply stopping the flow of immigrants (and the money they make for big business) is not a politically-viable option. Most voters are in the middle—in favor of legal immigration, including accepting legitimate refugees, with prescribed limitations, such as numerical quotas per year.

It is best to press candidates on their stance on immigration and, if they have held office previously, examine their voting record to see if they fulfill their promises. Immigration is a loaded subject and political candidates may be worried about coming off as unlikeable or overly harsh. But it is important to know where they stand on issues as important as our borders and the protection of the American labor class. No national-level candidate should be able to get your vote without having a firm answer on the subject, one way or another.

CHAPTER 12

THE ECONOMY

"Our economy is the result of millions of decisions we all make every day about producing, earning, saving, investing, and spending."
—President Dwight D. Eisenhower

Though it was not long ago, it is hard to remember late 2019 and early 2020 when some argued that our economy was the best it had ever been with only increasing success in sight. But then, the Coronavirus Pandemic came, and everything simply stopped. Businesses were closed, many of them forever, and its workers sent home. In the U.S., most citizens were sent one or two $1,200 stimulus checks along with the option of expanded unemployment benefits.

Under the circumstances, the stimulus payments seemed reasonable. Many Americans were unable to earn a living, so the government provided a safety net for its citizens. However, stimulus payments alone do not necessarily lead to productivity gains or economic growth. Hence it is often colloquially referred to as "printing money," and it is one of the factors that causes inflation. Said differently, having more money available without an accompanying increase in the supply of goods to spend it on can lead to increased prices and currency devaluations.

Our current economic malaise is also being driven by other factors, of course. The Fed kept interest rates artificially low in an attempt to encourage Americans to buy housing and other big-ticket items; supply chain issues created skyrocketing prices for basic goods; and we have already discussed how American energy production has decreased, while its consumption has increased, thus making the war in Ukraine a serious problem for gas prices.

In 2008, comedian Chris Rock made a joke that people were having to make life decisions at the gas pump. It is a comedian's job to help us laugh at the hard times, of course, but there are few things less funny than a working parent spending over half their paycheck on a tank of gas for a car they need to get to a job whose wages have not increased at the same rate as inflation even though the prices for everything else they need have. That was true in 2008 and it is even more true now.

Some of the issues in this book were important to include because many of us don't give them too much thought when the election cycle comes around. However, the economy does not fall into the category of overlooked issues. How could it? Every second of our lives is dictated by economic forces and we feel every minor downturn, especially for those in the working and lower classes. People who are able to just scrape by in a good economy face utter devastation in a recession.

Politicians are aware of this, of course. Democrat strategist James Carville famously said to Bill Clinton during his first presidential campaign, "It's the economy, stupid!" That is what Clinton focused on, and that is what got him elected. His personal charisma helped, to be sure, but it was his ability to speak to ordinary Americans about what they needed from the president. And he was able to deliver it as well.

So why do we have economic downturns if our leaders know they could be out of a job if they don't keep our economy strong? Unsurprisingly, the answer is complicated.

The Deficit: What is it and Why Does it Matter?

When speaking of the U.S. economy, the national debt level is often brought up in terms of measuring our economic health. But what exactly is it? And does it affect the lives of everyday Americans? The national debt level of the United States is simply a measurement of how much the government owes its creditors.[xc] The reason we have a national debt is because the U.S. government spends more money than it takes in from taxes and other income sources. As such, the national debt has continued to rise since it was last balanced in the 1990s.

As of February 2022, the national debt was thirty trillion dollars, a number so massive it is difficult to wrap our heads around it. Typically, when discussions about the national debt come up, politicians often argue, "You are sentencing our grandchildren to a lifetime of taxation." The reason the national debt keeps rising is no mystery: politicians spend money on programs for which they do not have funding in their current budgets. The expenses associated with these programs add to the national deficit, making it a problem for later. But it is still a problem, make no mistake.

There are at least five ways in which the national debt affects the American taxpayer:

- *First, as the national debt per capita increases, the likelihood of the government defaulting on its debt service obligation increases; this reduces the amount of tax revenue available to spend on other governmental services because more tax revenue will have to be paid out as interest on the national debt. Over time, this shift in expenditures will cause people to experience a lower standard of living, as borrowing for economic enhancement projects becomes more difficult.*

- *Second, as the rate offered on treasury securities increases, corporations operating in America will be viewed as riskier, necessitating an increase in the yield on newly issued bonds. This, in turn, will require corporations to raise the price of their products and services to meet the increased cost of their debt service obligation. Over time, this will cause people to pay more for goods and services, resulting in inflation.*

- *Third, as the yield offered on treasury securities increases, the cost of borrowing money to purchase a home will increase because the cost of money in the mortgage lending market is directly tied to the short-term interest rates set by the Federal Reserve.*

- *Fourth, since the yield on U.S. Treasury securities is currently considered a risk-free rate of return, and as the yield on these securities increases, risky investments such as corporate debt and equity investments will lose appeal.*

- *Fifth, and perhaps most importantly, as the risk of a country defaulting on its debt service obligation increases, the country loses its social, economic, and political power. This, in turn, makes the national debt level a national security issue.*[xci]

This is important for everyone to keep in mind. Even though Vice President Dick Cheney famously said, "deficits don't matter"[xcii] when asked about spending on the Iraq and Afghanistan conflicts, be assured that they do, for all of us.

In many ways, our economy is heavily influenced by the decisions our government makes on our behalf, some of them direct and others not. For instance, many pundits blame the 2008 Recession on deregulation, laws that reduced oversight of Wall Street firms. There were obviously many other factors and many market commentators are quick to remind us that government regulations and overreach can also be destructive for the economy, and the everyday lives of Americans. The point here is simply to emphasize that the decisions of our government, and certainly those of the Federal Reserve Bank, have consequences for our economy.

Bipartisan Economic Solutions

Be advised that your candidate for Congress or the Senate may not have the power, even if elected, to ensure a steady economy. However, if candidates advocate for certain programs to be passed into law, or speak in favor of existing programs that may be canceled, it is important to ask how the candidate believes the program will be funded, not just this election cycle, but for the length of the program. No matter your party or your preferred candidate, it is important to realize that no matter how needed or virtuous a particular program is, the bill will eventually come due. The question is whether it is worth it for you. And if debt must be incurred to pay for the program your politician is proposing, is it worth having the next several generations paying for it?

Taxes

Taxes are inevitable and non-negotiable. Paying taxes is a rite of passage of sorts. Many recall receiving their first paycheck, thinking it would be, perhaps $300 for two weeks of part-time work. Except when we got paid, it was only $211, and our mom or dad explained the impact of taxes, much to our teenage discontent. So, it may surprise you to learn that income taxes were not always a part of American life. The Constitution gave Congress the power to impose taxes and other levies on the general public, but in the early days, those taxes and levies were for a specific expense, such as a war or infrastructure costs.[xciii]

The federal income tax as we now know it now was officially enacted in 1913 with the passage of the 16th Amendment. "The amendment was passed by Congress in 1909, ratified by the states, and took effect on Feb. 25, 1913. That first year, less than 1% of the population paid income taxes at the rate of only 1% of net income."[xciv]

Of course, income taxes are not all that we pay. Other taxes that come out of our check like Social Security taxes started in the 1920s and 30s, as well as the estate tax and the gift tax. In most states, we also have sales tax. Initially, there were no filing statuses, so married people paid the same as single people. The taxes we pay now are calculated on a progressive basis, meaning the lowest earners, as of 2021, pay 10% income tax and the highest earners pay 37%.[xcv]

Makers vs Takers?

There is a popular refrain regarding taxes and who needs to pay their "fair share," suggesting that certain members of our society do not. However, this perception arises from differences in the types of taxes and the rates at which certain types of income is taxed.

Most of us pay income tax at a certain percentage, which varies depending on how much we earn in a year. If you work for an employer, you receive a Form W-2 Wage and Tax Statement and pay a percentage of your income to the federal government, as well as the state government, if your state has income tax. Taxes are a touchy subject because, as we just mentioned, our federal programs are paid for with tax revenues. So if a new program is proposed, one that would benefit a certain segment of society, those people would not be pleased to have the program denied because the government has insufficient funds. "Just raise taxes!" some will demand. "The rich aren't paying their fair share anyway!" they would argue to anyone willing to listen.

The perception that the richest Americans pay less taxes stems from two primary factors: 1) the conflation of income tax with capital gains tax, and 2) the reality that large corporations and wealthy individuals have resources to offshore their earnings that the average citizen does not. Indeed, the top five percent of earners pay the majority of income tax collected (60%).[xcvi] However, income taxes are not the only types of taxes. Capital gains tax, for instance, are generally lower than income tax. That means people who have the resources to invest and earn profits from their investments get to keep more of their money than people who earn a wage through their labor. This reality likely contributes to the class-based conflict between the very wealthy and everyone else.

This conflict can be perfectly encapsulated by a 2021 Twitter exchange between billionaire entrepreneur Elon Musk and Democrat Representative Pramila Jayapal:

> *When Musk announced that he would pay $11 billion in taxes this year, Rep. Pramila Jayapal (D-WA) argued that he was still failing to fork over his fair share.*
>
> *"Elon Musk made $36 BILLION in one day, but wants to brag about paying an $11 billion tax bill," said Jayapal. "Oh yeah, he also added more than $270 BILLION in wealth just since the pandemic started. Time for the rich to pay their fair share."*
>
> *The comment came after Sen. Elizabeth Warren (D-MA) — another progressive legislator — slammed Musk earlier this month for "freeloading off everyone else" and benefiting from "the rigged tax code." Musk replied to Warren: "And if you opened your eyes for 2 seconds, you would realize I will pay more taxes than any American in history this year."*
>
> *Musk and Warren have been feuding for several days over their competing visions for the tax code — as well as the role of the federal government in American life.*
>
> *"She struck first," Musk said during an interview with The Babylon Bee. "Obviously. She called me a freeloader and a grifter who doesn't pay taxes, basically. And I'm literally paying the most tax that any individual in history has ever paid this year, ever."*
>
> *"And she doesn't pay taxes, basically at all. And her salary is paid for*

by the taxpayer, like me," Musk continued. "If you could die by irony, she would be dead. If irony could kill."[xcvii]

However, it is important to realize that not all of the richest Americans have Elon Musk's resume. There are many wealthy Americans whose wealth is inherited thus, they pay no income tax, only capital gains tax, on money they did nothing to earn. As such, many of the loudest critics who insist millionaires and billionaires don't pay enough taxes are not being completely forthright, but neither are those who insist a flat tax is the only just solution or that all wealthy Americans are job creators who drive economic growth.

Flat Tax Debate

The idea of a flat tax is one that is debated, usually during Republican primaries in presidential election years. Most recently, its champions have been Dr. Ben Carson (who was later appointed as the HUD Secretary under President Trump), Governor Mike Huckabee, and Senators Ron and Rand Paul, both of whom ran for president in different years. Despite its frequent occurrence in debates and its general popularity among the Republican base, no viable path toward a flat tax has been made in the U.S.

A flat tax is a consistent tax rate applied to all taxpayers regardless of their level of income. Dr. Ben Carson suggested a flat rate of ten percent during his campaign, but other candidates have suggested different rates (e.g., nine percent and five percent). Flat taxes are generally only proposed for income tax purposes, rather than sales or capital gains taxes. Some countries, like Russia for example, currently employ a flat tax system. They have done so since the fall of the Soviet Union in 1991.

Proponents of the flat tax say it is fair because everyone pays the same percentage of tax across the board. It is also simpler and would result in Americans spending less money on accountants and tax return preparation services to avoid running afoul of an ever-more complicated IRS tax code. As a matter of fact, it could remove the need for the IRS all together.

Detractors argue that a true flat tax only benefits the rich. For example, if a wealthy household pays ten percent in tax, that is a small percentage that doesn't affect their quality of life. On the other hand, for households that are in the lower middle class, ten percent of their income is what they pay on food, housing, or childcare. It makes a bigger difference and would affect their quality of life. However, it should be noted that most flat tax plans that have been proposed by candidates include an exemption for low-income taxpayers, the elderly, and the disabled. Senator Rand Paul's plan also included tax deductions and tax exemptions, which makes his plan more of a hybrid between progressive taxes and flat taxes.

The Tax Preparer's Lobby

The U.S. has used a progressive tax since it started using an income tax. It accommodates for income disparities and is, mostly, popular with the American public. So why is there a growing call for a flat tax at all? The progressive income tax increases as income (however measured) increases. It also allows for a multitude of exemptions and reductions as outlined by the Internal Revenue Service, so you get tax breaks for a variety of reasons ranging from buying a house, having a child or retrofitting your house with solar panels. People like it because it raises revenue by taxing those who can most afford to pay, and it gives rewards in the form of tax breaks for desirable behavior.

However, opponents cite several reasons to dislike the progressive tax and the complicated tax code and exemptions are among them. The system is so complicated, in fact, that an honest person could very well find themselves being audited because they potentially failed to comply with the letter of the law with IRS requirements. But that is an extreme situation. What happens more frequently is that taxpayers who are middle class and below may not have the money to pay for a full-time accountant and sometimes not even enough to pay for a tax preparation service. So, the government ends up retaining tax refunds that should rightfully have been returned to them.

The question then becomes should we be required to pay a full-time professional just to ensure we don't overpay on our taxes? Of course, the tax preparers lobby would respond with a resounding YES.

While those at the very top of the income scale technically pay a higher tax percentage, they are presumed to have the financial means to employ tax professionals who ensure they get every available tax break, meaning the rate of tax they actually pay may be far less than it otherwise would have been. Part of the reason our tax code remains progressive and complicated is that large tax preparation companies send lobbyists to Congress to ensure their business keeps thriving. And in some cases, they have been found to have done so unethically.

In March of 2022, The Federal Trade Commission filed a complaint against one of those large tax preparation companies, accusing it of using deceptive advertising, making it appear to customers that their paid tax preparation services were a free filing with the IRS. These allegations were made after years of complaints about the company's marketing practices and their active lobbying efforts against the IRS even offering free filing. In response, the company issued a statement saying it would vigorously challenge the complaint.

If you're a person who uses the free file program to file your taxes, you should know that its days might be numbered. "The IRS Free File Alliance is a private-public consortium launched by the IRS in 2003 in response to President George W. Bush administration's proposal to create no-cost online federal tax prep as part of broader efforts to improve government technology to take advantage of the internet."[xcviii]

Two large tax preparation companies announced they would leave the program "to focus on further innovating in ways not allowable under the current Free File guidelines."

This follows the city of Los Angeles' lawsuit in 2019 against those two companies for allegedly directing taxpayers away from free file options and toward the paid options.

> *"[The company] has for years defrauded the lowest earning 70 percent of American taxpayers — who are entitled under a private industry agreement with the IRS to file their taxes online for free using commercial products — by actively undermining public access to the IRS's 'Free File' program, while simultaneously employing deceptive and misleading advertising and design schemes intended to induce taxpayers into unnecessarily purchasing expensive [company] products," the city attorney's complaint against [the company] alleged.*

> *Like [it's competitor, the company] is also a big lobbying spender.*

> *[The company] has spent about $38 million on federal lobbying since 1998 with over $3.4 million in spending last year and $3.5 million in 2020. [The company's] corporate PAC, has also given political groups and politicians across the political spectrum hundreds of thousands of dollars each election cycle.[xcix]*

No matter your opinion on taxes, it would benefit every taxpayer to inquire whether their congressperson or senator accepts money from the tax preparer's lobby as, most can agree, their interests may not be aligned with the everyday taxpayer.

What the Right Wants

Republicans have traditionally been the party of lower taxes, particularly for businesses and job creators. However, the Republican party is home to a variety of opinions on taxes, ranging from the Libertarian-leaning Ron Paul who openly said, "Taxation is theft," to moderate candidates like Mitt Romney who expressed displeasure with Americans who paid no income tax, though it should be noted he has never advocated to raise taxes on those Americans.

Mainstream Republicans, however, do typically advocate for lowering the rate of the top tax bracket, though maintaining our current progressive tax.[c] They also generally advocate for no inheritance tax and lowering taxes and regulations on businesses, reasoning those businesses can hire more people if they spend less per employee. It is an oversimplification perhaps, but ideas on economic policy varies much more widely among lawmakers and candidates than perhaps it does for other issues.

What the Left Wants

Views about economics and taxation vary among Democrats as well. Some far-left candidates, such as Bernie Sanders, unapologetically espouse Socialist views and believe the state should operate and control the means of production. There are also some Democrats who believe in a wealth tax, which means that unrealized gains in a billionaire's stock portfolio should be taxed as income.[ci] But most Democrats do not subscribe to these extreme views. Instead, Democrats most often view taxation as a tool to not only fund social programs, but also to level the economic field. Some mainstream Democrats hold to the notion that no one should be allowed to be a billionaire, that those "excess" funds should be taxed to help those with less.[cii]

After the 2020 election, Democrats had control of the presidency and Congress, so their proposed tax plans after that point are a good metric by which to measure the average left-leaning politician's ideal plan for taxation. According to the Cato Institute, the proposed tax plan would prioritize:

Infrastructure. The main provisions are subsidies for infrastructure bonds, building rehabilitation, and the low-income housing tax credit (LIHTC). The LIHTC is an awful, fraud-ridden program that mainly benefits developers. That the tax bill would expand it by $29 billion illustrates the absence of evidence-based policymaking in Washington.

Green Energy. The main provisions are subsidies for electric utilities, biofuels, energy efficiency, and electric vehicles. The subsidies are mainly in the form of tax credits, which are nearly always complex and difficult to administer.

Safety Net. The main provisions would expand the child tax credit (CTC), the earned income tax credit (EITC), and the child and dependent care tax credit (CDCTC). The official score shows that three-quarters of CTC and EITC benefits are spending, not tax cuts.

Tax Increases. The $2.1 trillion in tax hikes include raising the corporate tax rate ($540 billion), raising taxes on business foreign operations ($424 billion), and raising income and capital gains taxes on individuals and small businesses ($1 trillion).[ciii]

Though the result of taking a percentage of income from all working Americans is the same for both parties, the end goal of each is different. This means it is up to you, the voter to choose candidates who best reflect your beliefs about where your tax money should be going. Of course, none of us get veto power over what our elected officials spend our money on. But candidates are usually very open about their views on taxation and how our tax dollars should be spent. Spend some time researching your current representatives and those running for office, making sure your vote is going to candidates whose views on taxing and spending aligns with your views.

CHAPTER 13

GUN CONTROL

★★★★★

"I do not believe in taking away the right of the citizens for sporting, for hunting and so forth, or for home defense.
But I do believe that an AK-47, a machine gun, is not a sporting weapon or needed for defense of a home."
—President Ronald Reagan

They just keep coming, don't they? One after another, mass shootings have become a regular fixture in the news cycle. In other countries, even those that permit private firearm ownership, mass shootings are extremely rare—isolated even. But not here. I am writing these words just a few days after the horrific shooting at Robb Elementary School in Uvalde, TX, where nineteen children and two adults were murdered by a rifle-wielding eighteen-year-old.

It comes directly on the heels of the mass shooting in Buffalo, NY, where an assailant with white-supremacist motives killed ten people as they were going about their daily errands. The one before that was in a church in Sacramento—four dead at the hands of a middle-aged man who seemed to have political motives regarding China and Taiwan.

The one and only thing these shooters—and all the ones before— have in common is that they are male. The motives range wildly from politics to racism, to plain old mental illness. Sometimes, like in Las Vegas and in Uvalde, no motive is even clear. The only thing that is clear to everyone—left, right, and center—is that something must be done to stop this, to root out this sickness that uniquely afflicts our country.

History of the Second Amendment

As discussed in an earlier chapter, the Second Amendment reads: "A well-regulated militia, being necessary to the security of a free state, the right of the people to keep and bear arms, shall not be infringed." In the simplicity of the wording lies the reasoning behind our relatively easy access to firearms in the United States when compared to most other nations. It is important to acknowledge that the phrasing reflects how different the country was at that time. Militias, for one, existed as separate entities from the official Army (called "the regulars") and were used for a variety of purposes from assisting the Army in battle or defending individual homesteads from attack.

That being said, it is equally important to note that the Second Amendment was designed to protect Americans from the government. A common refrain from opponents of private gun ownership is something along the lines of, "You're not going to shoot deer with an AR-15." While they are correct, that statement and similar refrains are not necessarily the focus of those who support the Second Amendment. The most passionate supporters of the Second Amendment are often those who believe that no government is virtuous, including ours.

Part of the British oppression of the American colonies involved disallowing the colonists to have weapons to defend themselves and their property, something the framers wished to prevent. As such, removing the right of ordinary Americans, or even passing restrictions on what kinds of weapons can be owned, is hotly debated and ardently challenged. And banning firearm ownership outright would require a Constitutional Amendment that revokes the Second Amendment. Even the most fervent supporters of doing so admit that outcome is unlikely.

Until recently, the judiciary treated the Second Amendment almost as a dead letter. In District of Columbia v. Heller (2008), however, the Supreme Court invalidated a federal law that forbade nearly all civilians from possessing handguns in the nation's capital. A 5–4 majority ruled that the language and history of the Second Amendment showed that it protects a private right of individuals to have arms for their own defense, not a right of the states to maintain a militia.[civ]

Thus, barring a Constitutional Amendment, most Americans will retain the right to purchase and own firearms.

Legal Gun Ownership

Gun ownership across states varies wildly based on the citizens who live (and vote) there as well as the governor and state legislative bodies. In 2022, Montana and Wyoming topped the list of states with the highest guns per capita ratio while Hawaii and Massachusetts had the fewest. Montana and Wyoming are generally Republican voting states while Hawaii and Massachusetts are solidly Democrat, and have been for a very long time. However, gun ownership is not merely reflective of politics. People in rural environments, regardless of politics, generally own more guns. Not to protect from the government, necessarily, but from the wildlife that may wander onto their property.

What may surprise you is that legal gun ownership is lower now than it was in the 1970s, when around fifty percent of households had firearms. In 2013, it was down to thirty-two percent.[cv] Despite the decline in legal gun owners, the rate of mass shootings and gun violence in general has risen significantly. This disparity is part of the reason pro-Second Amendment advocates immediately dismiss calls for gun control. They argue that the data shows clearly it is not the guns in and of themselves causing this horrific uptick in violence.

When gun control advocates attempt to find solutions to protect people from mass shooters or being caught in crossfire, they usually run into barriers, which causes a great deal of frustration with constituents on both sides. "Why aren't you doing something?" we all ask our elected officials. The reason new legislative proposals so often end in deadlock, with no solutions being implemented, is because opponents of new laws typically respond with a few, all-important questions: 1) Would the proposed law have prevented the most recent mass shooting that we are reacting to? 2) Are existing gun laws currently being enforced? 3) In acquiring the firearms used in a mass shooting, did the shooter obey current laws?

In most situations, the answer to *all* those questions is a resounding no. For some reason, that is inevitably where the conversation stops. One side proposes a new law, the other side halts it. Both sides tell their constituents they did their best. Another shooting comes along, and the process repeats. It has become a predictable cycle. However, some would argue that we should take solace in the fact that at least the conversations are happening when these types of mass shootings occur. Yet, there are other senseless shootings that occur with regularity and often go uncovered in the national media. It appears no one tries to stop them and no one wants to engage in serious conversations to prevent them.

Illegal Guns

There is an interesting quirk in the data used for mass shootings. Anything with more than three victims in a single instance is deemed a mass shooting. But for some reason, the frequent crime-oriented shootings that do indeed include more than three victims at a time, are excluded from the mass shooting statistics. On Memorial Day weekend in 2022, in a span of three days, forty-seven people were shot, nine of them fatally.[cvi] And all of the news coverage of that terrible spate of death was local. Good Morning America didn't cover it. Neither did CBS News Tonight. Why?

The young men of color in cities like Chicago, Los Angeles, and New York shooting at each other day after day never make the national news, unless a celebrity is involved. Neither do their relatives who mourn their deaths. Neither do the neighbors who live in fear that they will be caught in the crossfire. The guns they use are nearly universally acquired illegally.

Perhaps it is too bold a statement to make, but it is reasonable to assume that in the most dangerous neighborhoods in this country, existing gun laws are not being obeyed. In that case, why should we assume that simply passing another one will change anything?

"From My Cold Dead Hands": The Commitment to Self-Defense

The resistance to new gun laws, though generally voiced by Republicans, is echoed by gun owners who own firearms for home defense. To be clear, this view is shared by many Americans, irrespective of political affiliation. In the summer of 2020, during the Covid-19 lockdowns and the protests that swept through multiple cities in the aftermath of George Floyd's death, firearm sales increased dramatically, including in traditionally left-leaning city centers.[cvii] The reason is simple: Americans did not feel safe, and they did not trust law enforcement to protect them.

The mass shooting in Uvalde crystalizes the concerns raised by many gun owners. According to media reports, for an hour, while children were under attack, the police staged outside the school but failed to timely act to stop the shooter. Even worse, they allegedly threatened, tackled, and arrested parents who tried to enter the school to save their children. The first to enter to confront the shooter was an off-duty Customs and Border Patrol agent who, upon getting a phone call from his daughter from inside the school, got up out of the barber chair, took his barber's shotgun, and charged into the school.[cviii]

A good deal of the resistance to the idea of private gun ownership is that it is unnecessary and dangerous. Opponents contend that we have police to protect us, both our persons and our property, so letting individuals have guns is unnecessary. However, this view appears to be starting to sway, at least a little, with the understanding that when it matters most, there may be no one there to protect you or your loved ones. And, if help comes, it may not arrive fast enough.

The question then becomes how you can pass gun legislation that continues to allow Americans to defend themselves (both from criminals and from malicious government actors) while actively defending against incidents like these. The problem is, the most commonly suggested remedies are not likely to be effective:

> *This then leads us to look at the specific actions the Democrats wish to take. Banning "assault weapons" or "large capacity magazines" would be unlikely to prevent someone from committing a crime with another weapon — demonstrated by the occurrence of mass shooting events which use handguns or shotguns — while removing the right of the vast majority of law-abiding citizens who possess such weapons without incident. Imposing stricter background checks may seem more reasonable, but makes the flawed assumption that existing government systems are working — there are multiple cases where the perpetrators of mass shooting events obtained guns despite their legal inability to do so — while forgetting the fact that guns are available to those who seek them out.*
>
> *This is simply to say that the simplicity of the "commonsense" solutions proposed by Democrats ignore real data and real problems, often in favor of the apparent desire to act swiftly.*[cix]

It is also apparent that the complete lack of oversight or investigation that some hardliners on the right advocate for cannot be the solution either. There may be a good faith argument for complete deregulation in the economy but there is not one for firearms. We need laws to keep bad actors from walking into a store and buying a weapon that will allow them to kill dozens of people in a few seconds. We also need to ensure parents have the means to counteract an armed assailant coming after their children.

What Most Americans Believe

In 2021, Pew Research and Gallup did a comprehensive poll of Americans' attitudes toward guns, their ownership, and what laws should exist to regulate them.[cx]

It is a common refrain that "there are more guns than people in the United States," which is true by the way. But it is important to keep in mind that only legal gun owners admit to owning firearms. Roughly a third of U.S. adults say they personally own a gun, with four in ten saying they live in a household with a gun in it. It will surprise no one to hear there are marked differences in the rates of gun ownership based on political party. For instance, 44% of Republicans and Republican-leaning independents say they personally own a gun, compared with only 20% of Democrats and those who lean Democrat. Also unsurprisingly, far more people in rural areas own guns (41%) compared to those who live in cities (20%) or the suburbs (29%).

As for why these Americans choose to own a firearm, personal protection tops the list. In Gallup's 2019 poll, 63% of gun owners cited personal safety or protection as the reason they own a firearm. This was an open-ended question on the poll, meaning the respondents were not prompted to select from a pre-populated list. Other answers to the question included hunting (40%), recreation or sport (11%), or that they needed a gun for their line of work (5%).

Even in 2021, the year we had six mass shootings, less than half of Americans (48%) polled viewed gun violence as a very big problem in the country. By comparison, more Americans participating in that poll viewed the affordability of health care as a very big problem (56%). It is also significant that only 6% of survey respondents viewed gun violence as not a problem at all.

African Americans were significantly more likely to think gun violence is a very big problem (82%). This was by far the largest percentage of any racial or ethnic group. About six in ten Hispanic adults (58%) viewed it as a very big problem and 39% of White adults viewed gun violence this way. Asian Americans were not given a category due to having too small of a sample size.

Big cities tend to vote Democrat and tend to have more people of color than the suburbs or rural communities. They also tend to have the most gun violence. So it should not be a surprise that African American and Hispanic people view it as a bigger problem, as do Democrats and Democratic-leaning independents (73%). They see more of it and are affected by it (or know someone who is). Republicans and GOP leaners are more likely to be in the suburbs or rural communities, and thus do not see gun violence as a major problem (only 18% said it was).

Bipartisan Solutions—What Do We Do?

Sorting out solutions can be difficult because of the multifaceted nature of the problem. As we discussed earlier, the number of guns owned by Americans today is lower than it was in the 1970s. But the number of targeted mass shootings has increased, and the frequency has accelerated. Considering sociocultural issues, it has been observed that many of the young men who staged a mass shooting did not have a father in the home. Or if they did, the father didn't do much fathering. But not all mass shooters are young men. Should we blame the behavior of a fifty-year-old on his upbringing?

Among Republicans and Republican-leaning independents, views have shifted. Republicans are currently more likely to say gun laws should be less strict (27%) than stricter (20%). Conversely, a large majority of Democrats and Democratic leaners (81%) say gun laws should be stricter.[cxi] How do we split this difference?

The key is to realize that the poll Pew Research used included the phrases "more strict" and "less strict." But can we be assured each respondent had the same definition of those terms? Probably not. It is this type of vague phrasing that keeps Americans who want the same thing divided and provides politicians with a convenient excuse for their lack of accountability and bipartisanship.

That same poll had nearly half of Americans (42%) of both parties say that legal changes would have no effect on the number of mass shootings. But that is not necessarily so. Though the Second Amendment is clear about our right to bear arms not being infringed upon, the government already prohibits the average citizen from certain kinds of weapons. Fully automatic machine guns, rocket-propelled grenade launchers or any other anti-aircraft weapon, and heavy ordnances. As private citizens, we are not permitted to own these weapons.

Most Americans believe the average citizen should not have easy access to "assault-style weapons" but here's the thing, many of them don't fully understand what that includes. That is a failure of our leadership.

Legislators cannot be expected to be experts in all fields, but they should be expected to consult with experts. If a legislator deems the AR-15 to be too dangerous to be sold to the general public, they should speak to a firearms expert so they can explain how an AR-15's capabilities differ from a 9mm pistol. Both are semi-automatic firearms. Why should one be legal and one not? Range of fire? The ability to modify the weapon? It may seem like nitpicking, but I assure you, it is not. It is vital for legislators to ensure the laws they pass protect our rights to defend ourselves while also impeding bad actors.

A great many congresspeople and senators are lawyers or highly-educated professionals. It is not convincing to hear that it is simply too onerous for them to define why a particular firearm or weapon modification ought to be illegal. There could not be a more serious business than allowing Americans to protect themselves and ensuring our laws stand as that vital first defense against calamity. Right now, there's a lot of rhetoric on both sides of the political divide with not enough viable solutions.

Yes, our media, in some ways, fosters the type of isolated, atomized loner who is perpetually online, has precious few examples of virtuous manhood, and a lot of anger against "those people" who are "ruining our country." But our elected officials are not empowered to pass laws about what our media is allowed to cover. As a matter of fact, they are expressly prohibited from doing so. In decades past, when violent media like music and video games came up for discussion in Congress, many Americans rejected Congressional intervention as an affront to our freedoms.

So, what is Congress empowered to do? Most Americans in both parties favor restricting gun access to those with mental illnesses (85% of Republicans and 90% of Democrats support this) and requiring background checks at private gun sales and gun show sales (70% of Republicans, 92% of Democrats). Majorities in both parties also oppose allowing people to carry concealed firearms without a permit. Right now, concealed carry differs across states.

There is also legislation that can be passed that does not affect the sale or possession of guns. Why was the Uvalde shooter permitted to just waltz into a school he didn't go to, weapon in hand? The outside entrances (there were many) were mostly unlocked. The classroom doors DID NOT have locks on them. It may be true that parents do not wish schools to feel like prisons, but we have locks on the doors to our homes. Why do we not have them for schools?

Ben Shapiro is an Orthodox Jew and founder of the Daily Wire, a conservative outlet. In the wake of the Uvalde shooting, Shapiro made the following proposal, based on his experience as a religious Jew in the U.S.:

> *In the Jewish community, we have been doing this for literally decades at this point. Armed security guards, protocols on locked exterior doors, lockdown procedures and mechanisms for classrooms, fenced campuses are commonplace and well-accepted. Usually the response to this is, "But that's not normal." From the same folks who correctly point out that it is not normal for kids to have to undergo "run and hide" training for school shootings. If we're going to make things more abnormal, can we at least do effective things?*

It seems that protection should be a part of federal funds that go to each state's public schools. In terms of passing building inspections, safety measures against attackers could perhaps be added as a requirement.

A more divisive suggestion is to allow teachers and school officials to carry guns in schools, a measure supported by over sixty percent of Republicans. But Democrats only approve of it at a rate of twenty-four percent. Part of the reason for this is that views on guns are linked to gun ownership. Those Americans who know how to handle weapons correctly and safely are in favor of having more of them. Americans who do not own guns, have never handled one, and perhaps do not even know anyone who does tend to want there to be no guns allowed.

These are but a few solutions that most people agree on: the mentally ill should not be allowed to own firearms. People with a history of violence, including domestic violence, should not be able to own guns. Background checks, though not infallible, should be mandatory. But what we need is honesty about what needs to be done with guns to stem the tide of death. That means being honest about who is dying most frequently and which guns are being used to kill. It means examining who is getting access to guns, both legally and not, and how we can prevent bad actors from getting them. Simply passing more laws isn't enough if we are to be serious about addressing the issue.

What are we doing to enforce existing laws to prevent mostly African American children from being shot to death as their father buys them ice cream?

What specific mental illnesses should preclude a person from owning a gun? What "red flags" will be included in red flag laws that will most effectively keep innocent people from being killed?

These are serious questions with no quick answers. And when dealing with the broad sword of federal law, it is incumbent upon our lawmakers to commit to serious deliberation with a view towards developing effective bipartisan solutions. And it is incumbent upon voters to hold them accountable and ensure they honor their oath to perform their duties or identify someone else who will in the next election.

CHAPTER 14

DRUGS (USE AND ABUSE)

★★★★★

"I have absolutely no pleasure in the stimulants in which I sometimes so madly indulge. It has not been in the pursuit of pleasure that I have periled life and reputation and reason. It has been the desperate attempt to escape from torturing memories, from a sense of insupportable loneliness and a dread of some strange impending doom."

—Edgar Allan Poe

Drug use in America has grown exponentially in the last three decades. Around nine percent of the population admits to being regular drug users as of 2021. The rise in drug use should perhaps not be surprising, given the increased support of marijuana legalization in our society. Marijuana is the most frequently used drug in the United States and widely perceived to be a benign indulgence, not unlike alcohol. It is often perceived more positively than alcohol in terms of long-term health effects.

However, people who go on to use more potent drugs usually begin with marijuana as their "gateway" drug (70.3% in 2013).[cxii] Drug use has the highest usage rate between people in their late teens and twenties and is also increasing among people in their fifties and early sixties. How you feel about those statistics most likely correlates with the way you tend to vote.

Early Drug and Alcohol Laws

Throughout the existence of the United States, our legislators have passed many "vice" laws regarding the use and sale of drugs and alcohol. For example, Congress famously passed Prohibition laws in the 1920s to ban the production and sale of alcohol, but that was far from the first set of laws aimed at keeping Americans substance-free. Many drugs such as cocaine, heroin, and amphetamines were freely available in the U.S. in the 19th and early 20th centuries as over-the-counter medicines. Opiates were particularly popular among women in the middle and upper classes, as it was not socially acceptable for women to drink enough alcohol to become drunk. However, taking a nip of laudanum (for "nerves") was perfectly acceptable. Both opiates and coca-derived medications were made illegal by the Harrison Narcotics Act of 1914 to reduce rates of addiction that were sweeping through the population. Despite marijuana being relatively benign in comparison, it too was later outlawed in 1937, after it migrated from being mostly used by the lower classes into middle- and upper-class homes.[cxiii]

Vietnam and the Start of the Drug War

Though drugs have long afflicted our society, the government didn't start investing a great deal of resources (and political capital) into fighting drug use and distribution until the early 1970s. On the heels of the hippie era and the summer of love, where drugs became a symbol of rebellion, increased drug use started to have more negative effects for society as a whole. In 1971, President Nixon declared a war on drugs.

No matter your age, you have likely heard this phrase many times. Because of the disparate nature of policing, the war on drugs has garnered a suspect reputation at best due to perceptions of racism and political prejudice.

A top Nixon aide, John Ehrlichman, later admitted: "You want to know what this was really all about. The Nixon campaign in 1968, and the Nixon White House after that, had two enemies: the antiwar left and black people. You understand what I'm saying. We knew we couldn't make it illegal to be either against the war or black, but by getting the public to associate the hippies with marijuana and blacks with heroin, and then criminalizing both heavily, we could disrupt those communities. We could arrest their leaders, raid their homes, break up their meetings, and vilify them night after night on the evening news. Did we know we were lying about the drugs? Of course we did."

Nixon temporarily placed marijuana in Schedule One, the most restrictive category of drugs, pending review by a commission he appointed led by Republican Pennsylvania Governor Raymond Shafer.

In 1972, the commission unanimously recommended decriminalizing the possession and distribution of marijuana for personal use. Nixon ignored the report and rejected its recommendations.[cxiv]

Heroin among Vietnam veterans was used as a smokescreen to launch widespread drug enforcement policy in the U.S. This is despite that fact that U.S. soldiers who used heroin while deployed in Vietnam (where the drug was cheap and plentiful) generally did not lapse into addiction once they returned home. In fact, it has been reported that only five percent of surveyed veterans continued to use heroin once they returned from Vietnam.[cxv]

As they so often are, Americans' good will to help our veterans and other vulnerable populations were used to excuse bad policy and bad laws, ones that had far-reaching implications for America as a whole, and African Americans in particular.

Racist Policing and Policy (Crack vs. Powder Cocaine Sentencing)

Starting with President Nixon's 1971 declaration of a war on drugs, policing and the prison system changed substantially. Instead of being perceived as a vice or an unhealthy habit like drinking or gambling, drug use became perceived as a crime, something only bad people did. This was not a natural evolution of public opinion mind you, but seemingly a targeted government campaign that escalated into pop culture thanks to multiple presidents from both parties. Even if you weren't alive at the time, you are probably aware of President Reagan's "Just Say No" campaign as well as the more pop-culture-derived slogan: "Crack is whack." There was also the school program D.A.R.E., which involved police officers and teachers making presentations to young school children about drugs and the consequences of using them.

There are of course a small minority of people who actively endorse drug use, usually as part of religious ceremonies. But recreational use has its proponents too. However, a vast majority of people do not believe that drug use is healthy for a person's body, nor do they think open drug use is good for society in general. This is why blanket legalization of drugs is never a serious proposal from any political party, not even the Libertarians. It is also why drug facilitation programs like needle swaps and safe use zones are only implemented in the most liberal cities. The average American is simply not in favor of widespread drug use even if they occasionally partake themselves.

However, the average American also has a deep sense of fairness. And when they finally became aware of the longstanding disparities in sentencing for drug possession, opinions began to change. It just took a long time and multiple long-term studies to bring about change. In 1986, Congress passed the Anti-Drug Abuse Act, which established mandatory minimums for specific quantities of cocaine. They also established much tougher sentences for crack than powder cocaine.

This legislation was proposed in response to the very real crack epidemic that was sweeping the inner cities and absolutely decimating African American communities. The threat was real. Even if well-intended, the response did not help. It made it worse.

Because of its relative low cost, crack cocaine is more accessible for poor Americans, many of whom are African Americans. Conversely, powder cocaine is much more expensive and tends to be used by more affluent white Americans. Nationwide statistics compiled by the Sentencing Commission reveal that African Americans are more likely to be convicted of crack cocaine offenses, while whites are more likely to be convicted of powder cocaine offenses.

Thus, the sentencing disparities punishing crack cocaine offenses more harshly than powder cocaine offenses unjustly and disproportionately penalize African American defendants for drug trafficking comparable to that of white defendants. Compounding the problem is the fact that whites are disproportionately less likely to be prosecuted for drug offenses in the first place; when prosecuted, are more likely to be acquitted; and even if convicted, are much less likely to be sent to prison.

Recent data indicates that African Americans make up 15% of the country's drug users, yet they comprise 37% of those arrested for drug violations, 59% of those convicted, and 74% of those sentenced to prison for a drug offense. Specifically with regard to crack, more than 80% of the defendants sentenced for crack offenses are African American, despite the fact that more than 66% of crack users are white or Hispanic.[cxvi]

Instead of convincing African American children not to use or sell crack, they were instead motivated to view the police as their enemy as great swaths of their communities were thrown in jail for unfathomably long times, while white, wealthy Americans possessing the same quantities of powder cocaine were given mere slaps on the wrist.

Over time, the media began to move away from their sensational crack hysteria coverage and start to listen to the people who had been affected by the drug war, as well as to chemists. It was difficult to ignore the lack of credible scientific evidence that could justify the vastly different sentencing for two forms of the same drug.

Though federal courts rejected arguments by defendants that the Anti-Drug Abuse Act violated the 14th Amendment's Equal Protection Clause, the disproportionate effect on African American defendants became a rallying cry for many activists on both sides of the aisle.

It took several pieces of legislation to do away with the mandatory minimum sentences as well as the differing sentences for powder versus crack cocaine, the most recent of which was in 2010. "President Obama signed the Fair Sentencing Act of 2010, doing away with the five-year mandatory minimum for possession of five grams of crack cocaine, and increasing the amount of crack required to result in a mandatory sentencing for federal drug trafficking crimes. The 2010 Act changed the ratio of crack to powder cocaine (for purposes of imposing the same sentence for possession of each form of the drug) from 100-to-one to 18-to-one."[cxvii] But drug arrests and jail sentences remain disproportionately high for people of color, even with a more liberal overall perception of drugs and people who use them.

Modern Usage and the Effect on Poor and Working-Class Communities

Like crack before it, working-class communities are being afflicted by yet another drug epidemic, only this time in opioid form. No matter their form, opioids are highly addictive. Despite this reality, starting in the late 1990s, pharmaceutical companies made it a staple of their prescription medication sales pitch that patients would not become addicted to prescription opioid pain relievers. This resulted in many more doctors being willing to prescribe them at higher rates. Predictably, this led to widespread misuse of these medications, being sold to people outside of medical practice, before finally coming to the attention of lawmakers when large numbers of previously productive members of society became addicted to drugs.[cxviii]

In 2017, more than 47,000 Americans died because of an opioid overdose, including prescription opioids, heroin, and illicitly manufactured fentanyl, a powerful synthetic opioid. Fentanyl is so powerful in fact, that in March of 2022 it was widely reported that two college boys died from a fentanyl overdose—not by taking the drug, but by performing mouth to mouth resuscitation on their friend who had taken it and stopped breathing.

However, some have argued that these claims may be overblown,[cxix] and it would be wise for lawmakers not to fall into the same trap they did with the crack epidemic—passing reactionary laws that do nothing to help the actual problem. Another difference about the modern opioid crisis is that it does not seem to favor one ethnic group over another. In the U.S. (as of 2020), deaths from opioid overdose reflected the overall population. For instance, white people were 69% of U.S. opioid deaths and Black (non-Hispanic) deaths were 17%.[cxx] These percentages are reflective of the overall ethnic makeup of the U.S. But it is hardly something to brag about. As a nation, our illicit drug use is increasing across all groups, and finding policy solutions that help rather than hinder is important.

What has been made very clear is that prison does not help stem drug use or its distribution. However, there are industry-recognized practices for drug addiction, including Cognitive Behavioral Therapy and the disease model of addiction. Regardless of the school of thought, addiction practitioners are united in the conclusion that prison, even those with drug programs, are not particularly helpful with helping inmates achieve long-term sobriety. The question then becomes what role should the criminal justice system play in possession offenses? To be clear, most Americans have no qualms with the current solution of sending drug distributors and dealers to prison.

Prisons in the United States do not have the capability to rehabilitate inmates that are incarcerated for drug use. Prisons have had the issue of overcrowding since the war on drugs began in the 1970s and partly due to the overcrowding issue, they simply do not offer the services needed for addiction rehabilitation.

Legalization? How the Parties Treat Drugs Now

Most of the conversation around legalization of drugs centers on marijuana, as there is not much of an appetite to make heroin, methamphetamine, or cocaine more easily accessible. This is especially true considering recent fentanyl-induced deaths that have been sweeping through the country. However, it has proven difficult for legislators to justify why marijuana specifically should be illegal while alcohol and cigarettes are not.

On the federal level, marijuana remains illegal. However, throughout the 2000s and 2010s, the decriminalization of marijuana has slowly been implemented on the state level. In fact, nineteen states and the District of Columbia have already legalized the drug for recreational use. As of 2018, 51% of Republicans disagreed with legalizing marijuana, 68% of independents agreed with legalizing, and 69% of Democrats agree with legalizing the drug. In 2022, a YouGov poll (which did not have breakouts for political party) found that a full 70% of Americans supported full legalization, rather than just for medical use.[cxxi]

Though Republicans have traditionally been less in favor of legalizing marijuana, their views are also changing. In addition, rather than being concerned about the potential harm that could be caused by legal and readily available marijuana, much of the opposition is now focused on whether the industry should be subsidized by taxpayers. It may seem a cold calculation when speaking about the effect drugs have on our communities and our lives, but these are conversations we must have. Also, when evaluating our lawmakers' performance and the vision of prospective candidates, we would be wise not to overlook or undervalue the importance of asking where our tax dollars are being deployed. Ask the tough questions and the conversation may not always be comfortable!

- Is my elected official voting to spend my tax dollars on effective drug policy?
- Do legislators believe we should subsidize the drug industry? And, if so, under what circumstances?
- Are the programs my legislators are supporting helping my community?
- Are lawmakers working with medical and regulatory bodies to discern between drug users who may need help and drug dealers who are violating the law?

Asking these questions helps to focus our attention on what the government can do to reduce the flow of drugs and the adverse impact they have in our communities. No government can completely eradicate the availability of drugs or other intoxicants. Many have tried and they have all failed. Voters should continue to press lawmakers to ensure they are acting in the best interest of their constituents.

CHAPTER 15

ABORTION

"Pro-choice and pro-life activists live in different worlds, and the scope of their lives, as both adults and children, fortifies them in their belief that their own views on abortion are the more correct, the more moral, and more reasonable."
—Kristin Loker

In May of 2022, a leaked Supreme Court draft opinion written by Justice Samuel Alito foreshadowed that the landmark Supreme Court decision in Roe v. Wade would soon be overturned. In Roe v. Wade, the Court ruled that abortion was a constitutionally protected right.[cxxii] For over fifty years, that was the established law of the land. As such, neither supporters nor opponents likely believed Roe v. Wade would ever be overturned. No doubt, the leaked opinion was a huge shock to everyone, but the Supreme Court made it official on June 24, 2022, in the case of Dobbs v. Jackson Women's Health Organization.

Since 1973, when Roe v. Wade was decided, the issue of abortion has been a flashpoint in American politics, starkly dividing the two major parties, churches, communities, and even personal relationships.

To be clear, the Court's decision to overturn Roe v. Wade does not outlaw abortion in the U.S. Rather, it leaves the decision to each state to determine whether, and under what circumstances, abortion will be permitted within its borders. More specifically, it allows the residents of each state to vote on whether they want it available and in which terms of pregnancy. Thirteen states already had "trigger laws" on the books, meaning that the second Roe v. Wade was overturned, abortion became illegal in those states (Arkansas, Idaho, Kentucky, Louisiana, Mississippi, Missouri, North Dakota, Oklahoma, South Dakota, Tennessee, Texas, Utah, and Wyoming). Other states have already announced the issue will be on the ballot.

Pro-life advocates are predictably pleased by these events. Just as predictably, pro-choice advocates are displeased, to say the least. It seems that no matter what federal and state legislatures decide on the abortion issue, anger and division will likely follow. But why does this particular issue evoke so much emotion? Other hot button issues exist of course, but none seemingly to this degree. Perhaps there is a simple reason for the escalated tension: no matter who you ask or what side they are on, everyone will tell you abortion is the main dividing issue in our country because there are lives at stake. Millions of them. The heart of the disagreement centers on *which* lives. And that is a chasm that is not easily crossed.

Before Roe v. Wade: Abortion in the U.S.

Before the Roe v. Wade decision, abortion was legal in the U.S. on a limited basis. Thirty states outlawed abortion under all circumstances (for elective abortions). However, twenty states permitted abortions in certain circumstances:

In 1967, Colorado became the first state to decriminalize abortion in cases of rape, incest, or in which pregnancy would lead to permanent physical disability of the woman. Similar laws were passed in California, Oregon, and North Carolina. In 1970, Hawaii became the first state to legalize abortions on the request of the woman, and New York repealed its 1830 law and allowed abortions up to the 24th week of pregnancy. Similar laws were soon passed in Alaska and

Washington...By the end of 1972, 13 states had a law similar to that of Colorado, while Mississippi allowed abortion in cases of rape or incest only and Alabama and Massachusetts allowed abortions only in cases where the woman's physical health was endangered. In order to obtain abortions during this period, women would often travel from a state where abortion was illegal to one where it was legal.[cxxiii]

The issue of whether abortion should be a state or federal issue is very often argued from the perspective of poor women or those who are otherwise marginalized. For pro-choice women seeking an abortion, those with the financial resources to travel to other states or even other countries were still able to have the procedure. Feminist icon Gloria Steinem famously traveled to London in 1957 for an abortion, an experience she detailed in her autobiography and more recently on National Public Radio (NPR).[cxxiv] However, not all women had the funds or ability to travel to another state to have the procedure done, assuming they even had the funds for the procedure in the first place. Advocates for making abortion a federal right often point to the reality that women who have the most dire consequences from unplanned or unwanted pregnancies are the same women who do not have the ability to travel to receive one.

Byllye Avery is a health care activist. She has been working on reproductive rights issues since 1971.

At the time, women would also travel to terminate their pregnancies abroad or to New York, where abortions were legalized in 1970. But Avery says that kind of travel just wasn't possible for many women she counseled in Florida, where the procedure was illegal in most cases.

"A Black woman came, and we started giving her this information. She said: 'I don't have any money to go to New York. I don't know

anybody there.' And about a month or two later, she died from a self-induced abortion. So that really opened my eyes that, even if we had access to abortion, they still didn't really have access. "[xxv]

These were the cases abortion advocates pointed to when seeking legal redress. Ultimately, the Supreme Court, as it was in 1973, agreed, passing Roe v. Wade into law. It's hard to speculate what those justices imagined would happen to the controversy surrounding abortion. But if any of them imagined the ruling would end the debate, I think it is fair to conclude that they were quite mistaken.

After Roe

Once abortion was ruled a constitutional right, opponents of abortion were galvanized not only to see Roe overturned, but also to go directly to the American people to tell them about what abortion was and why it was morally wrong. Most pro-life activists were some denomination within Christianity, with a small minority being members of other faiths and even some non-believers. When Roe was decided, the U.S. was mostly a Christian nation. However, as decades passed, fewer and fewer Americans identified as belonging to a specific religion, setting the majority of the pro-life movement at odds with the general American public.

The Pro-Life Movement

Those who oppose abortion believe that human life begins at conception. Once an egg is fertilized, they argue, it becomes a separate and unique human life from that of the mother. Even before it can feel pain, even before it can live and breathe on its own outside the mother's body. It is a person and has all the rights that a baby outside the womb does. In order to communicate that message, a common tactic was to bring graphic pictures of aborted fetuses to protests. Not only outside abortion clinics, but also outside lawmakers' offices. The actual procedure of abortion is rather gruesome, and the pictures, particularly those of abortions in the second and third term were horrific. They were intended to be. But instead of galvanizing the people who saw those pictures, they alienated the people they were hoping to persuade.[cxxvi]

Many pro-life tactics were drawn from John and Barbara Willke's *Handbook on Abortion*, which many called the "Bible of the pro-life movement."

> *The Willkes were a Catholic couple, a doctor and a nurse, who became convinced that pictures would help end legal abortion. ... They became sure that images helped people to understand a fetus, legally and culturally, as a baby. Thus, the movement continued to develop new tools and technologies to this end: pictures of fetuses, in utero and aborted, fetal models, and fetuses in jars in the 1970s; fetal pins, dolls, jewelry, and clothes in addition to a proliferation of pro-life movies in the 1980s; and ultrasound visuals of fetuses in the 1990s and 2000s. Using these images, activists made a political pitch and moved fetal bodies squarely into American political culture.*[cxxvii]

With most of the movement operating from the same playbook, the harder the pro-life movement pushed this image, the less it worked. Pro-choice advocates kept their focus on the mothers—poor women, women who had suffered rape, barely pubescent victims of incest, and women who lived in abusive relationships. These stories were far more compelling to the average American than the gag-inducing photos of the results of abortions.

Unfortunately, the negative opinion of pro-lifers did not come solely from the protests with unsavory photos on poster board. Before the 20th century was over, it would get far, far worse, smearing the pro-life movement as well as American Christianity as a whole.

Many evangelical laypeople and clergy opposed legal abortion and joined the fight to end it. Some simply joined existing pro-life groups; others formed new, more radical groups that rejected the politics of legislative reform. The most famous of the latter cohort was Operation Rescue, which sought to end abortion by "any means necessary." Operation Rescue pioneered the pro-life "rescue," in which thousands of activists created human blockades in front of clinics.

In the 1980s and 1990s, Operation Rescue performed such rescues in cities across the nation, tying up the city's police departments, filling local jails, and making it incredibly difficult to get an abortion. Their national media spectacle sought to attract reporters and stun the American public. Extremists in the movement went even further. Between the early 1980s and the 2000s, there were 153 assaults, 383 death threats, 3 kidnappings, 18 attempted murders, and 9 murders related to abortion providers.[cxxviii]

Though the debate around abortion was only becoming more fierce as we entered the 21st century, the overreach of the loudest pro-life activists seemed to push popular perception to be at least moderately pro-choice. In his first presidential campaign, Democrat President Bill Clinton famously said abortion should always be "safe, legal, and rare,"[cxxix] a sentiment, it seemed, the majority of Americans agreed with. But with the new millennium came different messaging from the pro-choice camp and with it, a turning of the tide.

Modern Activism

Democrat and Left-Wing Activism

Though polls continued to show the majority of Americans approved of some access to abortion, the tone of pro-choice activism began to change (as so many things did) around 2014. The messaging changed from "safe, legal, and rare" to "Shout your abortion"[cxxx] and an increase in demand for government-funded abortion by repealing the Hyde Amendment, which prohibits taxpayer money from being used for abortion. But turning the very personal, often traumatizing decision of women who feel they have nowhere to turn into a celebratory social media campaign did not seem to sit well with some, even those who identified as pro-choice.

Even famed atheist Christopher Hitchens challenged this narrative before his death. In one of his many public addresses, he stated: "You see a woman kicked in the stomach. Your instinct is properly one of revulsion. You learn that the woman is pregnant. Who will reply that this discovery does not multiply their revulsion?"[cxxxi] Displeasure at the tactics of activists (generally) did not turn pro-choice people into pro-life people. But it did seem to deepen the fissure that existed in the stark dichotomy: Pro-choice or Pro-life.

That fissure would rupture wide open leading up to the elections in 2020. Activists are one thing and it is often easy to dismiss them. However, when lawmakers get involved, it tends to have a chilling effect on voters, particularly those suburban moms who so heavily sway elections.

In 2019, Virginia Governor Ralph Northam appeared on a morning radio show while campaigning for reelection. The radio host asked him if he supported proposed legislation that would permit abortion for a woman in labor. He stated:

> When we talk about third-trimester abortions, these are done with the consent of the mother, with the consent of physicians, more than one physician by the way, and it's done in cases where there may be severe deformities, there may be a fetus which is non-viable. So in this particular example, if the mother is in labor, I can tell you exactly what would happen, the infant would be delivered, the infant would be kept

comfortable, the infant would be resuscitated if this is what the mother and the family desired, and then a discussion would ensue between the physician and the mother.[cxxxii]

Hearing that a far-left activist would advocate for leaving a viable baby to die would likely not have ruffled feathers of some people. But hearing an elected Governor saying such a thing was rather shocking, even to many pro-choice proponents. Conservative outlet the Daily Wire, in an article by founder and editor at large Ben Shapiro, had this to say about Northam's statement:

> *This is pure infanticide. It's also an argument for eugenic murder (see his comments about deformities). Northam is specifically talking about delivering an infant alive and then asking the mother whether the infant should live or not. This is not an argument about the morning-after pill. It's not an argument over whether a fetus feels pain. This is a statement that a fully-formed infant, born alive, ought to be murdered if the mother says the infant ought to be murdered.*
>
> *This is pure evil.*[cxxxiii]

Though it was heavily speculated that Northam lost his subsequent gubernatorial race to Republican Glen Youngkin over the issue of schools (as we discussed in a previous chapter), there were several campaign ads about Northam's statement about a baby born alive leading up to the election. It was seemingly a message the people of Virginia rejected.

That same year, a You.gov poll found that seventy-nine percent of *pro-choice* respondents opposed late-term abortions and eighty percent opposed day-before-birth abortion.[cxxxiv] Pro-choice Americans, it seemed, did not feel like their interests were being represented by their leaders.

Republican and Right-Wing Activism

Seeming to have learned the lessons of previous decades, Conservative, Christian, and Republican messaging on abortion became more centered on the woman and the effect of the procedure on her. In many circles, it also decoupled the morality questions from Christianity, as many Americans no longer identify as belonging to a particular religion. Even if they do, their religion does not necessarily inform their opinion on civil policy.

In addition to religious entities, millennial activists like Lila Rose of Live Action and Abby Johnson have been front and center, speaking directly to women in ways older generations did not. Johnson in particular is notable as she was not only previously pro-choice, but also worked in a Planned Parenthood facility and assisted with abortions.

Additionally, conservative news outlets have focused on the issue, opposing the notion that women are better served by having abortions. Daily Wire personality Michael Knowles reported on a horrific story in Ohio in which a ten-year-old child had to leave the state to procure an abortion. Because Ohio's existing laws would have allowed the child to get an abortion due to her age and inability to carry a baby to term, reporters investigated more thoroughly. As ten-year-old children cannot consent to sexual activity, they concluded that she must have been the victim of a crime.[cxxxv]

This case (and the unacceptably high number of cases like it) stood in rebuke of the push to allow minors to obtain abortions without parental consent. Taking such action would inevitably conceal crimes. Who has fathered the child with the ten-year-old? If another minor, then who is paying for the abortion? Luckily, in this case, all involved acted in the best interest of the victimized child. She received treatment and her abuser was arrested and incarcerated.

Finally, some contend that ever-increasing technological advancements have added credence to the pro-life contention that the fetus is a person separate from the mother, and therefore entitled to their life. Though the majority of Americans still favor access to abortion in some cases (specifically, rape, incest, and to save the life of the mother), there is less agreement among voters regarding the how far into a pregnancy should abortion be permitted.

Abortion and the African American Community

When speaking about African American women and abortion, Democrat lawmakers often mistakenly assume that all African American voters support their position. However, as we have already discussed, that is not the case. The majority of African Americans are or lean towards voting Democrat, but it is far from universal. Like all other ethnic groups, there is a divide between the two parties in the African American community.

Attitudes Toward Abortion Over Time: Black Democrats, Black Non-Democrats and Non-Black Democrats

Regardless of whether or not you think abortion should be legal, please tell me whether you personally believe that in general abortion it is morally acceptable or morally wrong.

Do you think abortions should be legal under any circumstances, legal only under certain circumstances or illegal in all circumstances?

	Abortion: % Morally acceptable		Abortion: % Legal under any circumstances	
	2001-2007	2017-2020	2001-2007	2017-2020
Black Democrats	34	50	27	35
Black non-Democrats	20	34	11	22
Non-Black Democrats	53	66	36	45

GALLUP

Source: Gallup, 2020

As we can see in the 2020 Gallup poll, there was nearly a twenty percent difference in the number of African American Democrats who found abortion to be morally acceptable and African Americans who were not Democrats. Likewise, there was a thirteen percent difference between African American Democrats and African American non-Democrats regarding whether abortion should be legal under any circumstance.

That breakdown is particularly helpful, because when Gallup groups all African Americans together in that same poll, the numbers do not appear to be as nuanced. The 2020 Gallup poll measured Black Americans' perceptions regarding abortion in comparison to Americans who were not Black. In answering the question: "Regardless of whether or not you think abortion should be legal, please tell me whether you personally believe that in general abortion it is morally acceptable or morally wrong," forty-six percent of Black Americans answered that it was morally acceptable. This is very similar to the rate of non-Black Americans, forty-three percent of whom answered in the affirmative. There was a much bigger difference in percentages for the question, "Do you think abortions should be legal under any circumstances, legal only under certain circumstances, or illegal in all circumstances?" For this question, only twenty-seven percent of non-Black Americans answered that it should be legal under any circumstances. However, thirty-two percent of Black Americans answered that it should.

When it comes to having abortions, Black women are massively over-represented in several states, including Alabama (62%), Georgia (65%), and Mississippi (74%).[cxxxvi] In looking at these states, it's not hard to see a pattern. They are all southern states with relatively high rates of poverty. Additionally, as of 2020, seventy percent of Black babies were born to unmarried mothers.[cxxxvii] So it stands to reason that the high percentages of Black women seeking out abortions in these areas have a social cause: single, often poverty-stricken women without community resources, perhaps who are even underage in some cases.

Though some would argue it is not merely a matter of lower socioeconomic status that has driven the outsized proportion of Black women having abortion.

The prevalence of abortion facilities within minority communities serves as a major contributor to the rate in which black women obtain abortions. Accordingly, black women are 5 times more likely to have an abortion than white women. A recent study released by Protecting Black Life, an outreach of Life Issues Institute concluded that, "79% of Planned Parenthood's surgical abortion facilities are strategically located within walking distance of African and/or Hispanic communities." This study coincides with historical revelations that eugenicists dating to the mid-1900s, "[argued] that the most effective way they could advance their agenda would be to concentrate population control facilities within targeted communities."[xxxviii]

Given the ugly history of eugenics and what has been alleged about Margaret Sanger, the founder of Planned Parenthood, the concentration of clinics is indeed noteworthy, and not just by pro-life advocates.

What Voters Can Do

With legislation in the works at the state level, it is important for citizens to vote for amendments and other initiatives when placed on the ballot. For those states that have laws already on the books regarding abortion, then it comes down to determining if your incumbent representatives are still serving your interests. As we saw with the shift in messaging from the 20th to the 21st century, who you elect to represent your voice does not necessarily need to be an extreme "no-abortion" or "abortion-til-birth" choice. Especially during the primaries, you can (and should) pay attention to candidates' views and voting records, and then vote for those who reflect your values.

Like any other issue in politics, it can feel like your voice is being drowned out by extremists on both sides. But it is the regular voter who holds the power, that is the true majority. All it takes is engagement and careful listening on your part. Then, at least on a local level, you can be sure to have the government that represents you and your values.

CHAPTER 16

URBAN AMERICA (FIXING OUR INNER CITIES & BLACK-MAJORITY CITIES)

"By far the greatest and most admirable form of wisdom is that needed to plan and beautify cities and human communities."
—Socrates

The pandemic and associated lockdowns, in a way, redefined our society—the way we went about our work, schooling, and certainly where many chose to live. Large city centers have always been a double-edged sword, offering both high culture that drew people in by the millions (both to live and to visit) as well as higher tendency toward crime and violence.

But after the lockdowns, many people in large urban centers found that without access to restaurants, theaters, and other social activities, the city they lived in suddenly seemed old, dirty, cramped, and in some neighborhoods, dangerous. This prompted a huge wave of relocations from all major cities in the U.S. Though many people moved to entirely different states, most did not. They just left the cities in which they were residing in search of comfort in the suburbs.

Moves out of the densest parts of big cities, those with more than 10,000 people per square mile, jumped 17% to about 2.9 million during the first year of the pandemic, from March 2020 to February 2021, according to the analysis. The number of moves out of those dense areas returned to pre-pandemic levels in the following year, March 2021 to February 2022.

Some areas of Florida, North Carolina, South Carolina and Texas swelled with out-of-state movers who left shutdown coastal cities in search of roomier, cheaper Sun Belt homes. However, many people who moved out of cities just headed for nearby suburbs within their state. [cxxxix]

But what about those who couldn't just pack up and move? Decades ago, inner cities experienced something called "white flight" wherein the previous white majority abandoned cities in favor of the suburbs, actively seeking to escape the burgeoning integration of the times. Now, something similar is happening. However, it is not a disdain for diversity that is leaving city centers mostly filled with African Americans and other people of color—rather it is often a lack of financial resources.

African Americans' Wealth and Home Ownership

Employment – The overwhelming majority of Americans gain wealth from income earned through labor. This is true for all ethnic groups. As such, unemployment rates are good indicators of the prosperity or lack thereof of America as a whole, or specific, targeted groups. Examining the unemployment rates for Black Americans, there has historically been higher unemployment among African Americans, even (or especially) among those living in cities with the highest concentration of Black residents.

- *While the African American unemployment rate is at or below its pre-recession level in 17 states (of the 22 states and the District of Columbia for which these data are available), in 14 states and the District of Columbia, African American unemployment rates exceed white unemployment rates by a ratio of 2-to-1 or higher.*

- *The District of Columbia has the highest black–white unemployment rate ratio overall, at 8.5-to-1, while South Carolina and Maryland have the highest ratios among states (3.2-to-1 and 2.8-to-1, respectively).*
- *The highest African American unemployment rate is in the District of Columbia (12.9 percent), followed by Illinois (9.1 percent) and New Jersey (9.0 percent). The highest Hispanic state unemployment rate is in Connecticut (10.0 percent). In contrast, the highest white state unemployment rate is 5.2 percent, in West Virginia.[cxl]*

The numbers above are from 2018, which is a few years ago and before the pandemic. The availability of more recent data depends heavily on what kind of surveys were performed during and after the widespread Covid-19 lockdowns. In February of 2022, The Center for New York City Affairs released unemployment data for Black New Yorkers and the results were startling. "One in five Black New Yorkers is either officially unemployed, stuck in a part-time job when they want full-time work, or so discouraged they are not even looking for employment—suffering the worst job hits of the pandemic recession."[cxli] That's more than fifteen percent unemployment among Black Americans living in New York City, one of the largest city centers in the U.S. and arguably the cultural and economic hub of our nation. It's also among our most diverse cities and has been governed nearly exclusively by Democrats for decades. As of 2021, the overall national unemployment rate for Black Americans was 6.3%, which is comparable for that of white Americans. So why is a city the size of New York doing so poorly?

It's hardly an isolated phenomenon. On the opposite coast in Los Angeles, Black unemployment was eleven percent in February 2022.[cxlii] Looking to the center of the country, in Chicago, it is also eleven percent.[cxliii] It is important to note that not all states and cities track unemployment by race. In fact, most do not. So the data set is incomplete and it is difficult to draw conclusions about how specific policies from local lawmakers directly affect the African American populace. But in looking at the states that do track the racial breakdown, a clear pattern has emerged; African Americans are less employed than Americans of other races and, as such, have collectively far less wealth.

Business Ownership – Without first being an employee of a business, it is hard to imagine how one can become an owner of a business, so it will likely not be surprising that there also is a disparity in African American business ownership. Every year, the US Census Bureau conducts an annual business survey, the most recent of which was released in 2020. Subsequent surveys (collecting data from 2020 and 2021) were halted due to Covid-19, but they are expected to release a new one in 2023. In 2019, there were 134,567 Black-owned employer businesses (businesses with more than one employee) in all sectors of the U.S. economy, an eight percent increase from the 124,551 Black-owned employer businesses in 2018, according to the American Business Survey.

In 2018, there were about 3,115,000 nonemployer businesses with Black owners, which was almost a six percent increase from the 2,951,000 businesses in 2017, according to the Census Bureau's 2018 Nonemployer Statistics by Demographics (NES-D). It is a positive sign that these numbers are trending upward, but we can see that right now, only about two percent of businesses are Black-owned, which is abysmally low.[cxliv]

When considering our major industry players, the story gets no better. Even those African Americans who get a job and do well—about twenty percent of Black households nationwide bring in 100 thousand dollars a year or more[cxlv]—very few rise to the highest levels of their profession. In the entire history of the Fortune 500, for instance, there have only ever been nineteen Black CEOs of companies who made the list.[cxlvi]

Why do some African Americans do well, even when born into difficult circumstances, while many others struggle? Some of the most influential African Americans like Thurgood Marshall, Reginald Lewis, Colin Powell, Oprah Winfrey, Condoleezza Rice and Ben Carson grew up in poverty-stricken circumstances, racially segregated times or less than ideal situations. Yet they each overcame their circumstances and achieved great success and wealth! Does it really all come down to the individual? Is this about young African Americans simply not being willing to "pull themselves up by their bootstraps" while other races will?

Most will agree that the answer to that rhetorical question is no. Policy failures can and often do negatively impact our experiences on a broad scale and the impact is often exacerbated in minority-majority neighborhoods. High crime rates, failing schools, poor housing conditions (or unavailable housing in some cities) create a recipe for failure—in individuals and communities. We need look no further than the current state of some of our most populous cities for evidence of that.

Baltimore, Chicago, and Media Silence

The most glaring indication of a failing city is its level of crime. Inner cities nationwide have long had higher crime rates than suburbs and rural areas. But something noteworthy happened in 2020. After the death of George Floyd in Minneapolis, cities across the country burned. The riots spread far and wide, hitting affluent areas, most certainly. But the overwhelming majority of the damage occurred in city centers, many of which were Black-majority neighborhoods.

Despite months of violent crime that resulted in more than a billion dollars in damage,[cxlvii] there were very few consequences for the people (of all races) who did this. The perpetrators went largely unpunished. In some cases, the few who were arrested were bailed out by community donations supported by elected officials.[cxlviii] The actions and reactions created a paradox of sorts. Commit crimes in Black-majority areas and there will be no punishment, so long as you proclaim yourself to be in service of racial justice. And who are the ones to bear the burden of these policies? The African American families and business owners who live and work in these neighborhoods.

It is difficult to remain unmoved as you watch Black business owners spray paint their windows with messages saying, "Black owned, please don't burn" in the desperate hope that their livelihoods will not be destroyed.[cxlix] Because they know the violence is coming, and that no one will do anything about it. Does this inspire young African Americans to open a business? Does it inspire business owners of *any* race to open businesses in majority-Black neighborhoods? Does it inspire anyone to invest in those communities?

This refusal to enforce laws has taken on other forms as well. In California, they turned a blind-eye to theft, causing multiple chain-store businesses to close locations and leave.[cl] New York and Los Angeles have also seen an increase in crime, both violent and property-related, the majority of which are committed by and against African Americans and other people of color. Some argue that these circumstances are magnified by recent bail reform initiatives, which in some cases result in repeat violent criminals being arrested and released back out onto the streets again.[cli]

Policing and Race Relations – You might ask why politicians would pass laws supporting or encouraging this kind of behavior. In all cases, these bail reform initiatives and efforts to change felonies into misdemeanors is spearheaded by far-left Democrats. These are politicians who were elected because their constituents believed, rightly or wrongly, that they would be a better ally to people of color and other historically marginalized populations. Part of that marginalization and the very need for visible allyship is the complicated history of race-targeted police activity in the U.S. In response to that, and specifically the death of

George Floyd, many district attorneys, governors, and police chiefs came together in search of ways to reduce the overrepresentation of African Americans in the prison system.

Unfortunately, in trying to solve one problem, these civic leaders created another, much bigger one.

After a weekend in which three people were killed in Oakland, Calif., including a 1-year-old hit by a stray bullet while sleeping in the back seat of his mother's car, Mayor Libby Schaaf finally reversed herself on defunding the police and pledged to hire more cops. But what took her so long?

Murder rose by nearly 30% last year, and Americans have been making it as clear as can be that they want more and better policing. The incoming mayors of Atlanta, New York and Seattle ran campaigns that prioritized public safety. A ballot initiative in Minneapolis that would have dismantled the police department was defeated soundly, and some of the strongest opposition came from low-income black communities. "Black lives need to be valued not just when unjustly taken by the police, but when we are alive and demanding our right to be heard, to breathe, to live in safe neighborhoods and to enjoy the full benefits of our status as American citizens," explained a civil-rights activist from Minneapolis in a New York Times op-ed.[clii]

Arguments for defunding the police unambiguously hurt Black communities. Here are just a few examples of the results of such policies:

- In 2020, the Portland City Council voted to disband the city's Gun Violence Reduction Team. The homicide rate in Portland subsequently rose 800 percent. The majority of the victims were Black men.
- In Seattle, the city council ran out the department's first

female Black police chief, then cut the budget by twenty percent. As a result, officers quit the force in record numbers due to being painted as bigots and murderers. Seattle then saw a 26-year-high homicide rate. The Black population of Seattle is only seven percent. Despite this, Black victims accounted for forty-nine percent of Seattle homicides.

The Middle Way

Hardline law-and-order policies have, in the past, sometimes resulted in disparate sentencing for offenders (crack vs cocaine) and harassment of law-abiding citizens (stop and frisk). This does not serve Americans well, as has rightly been pointed out in the past. However, swinging wildly to the hardline leftist policies has not helped communities of color with the systemic issues plaguing them, as people are now seeing.

San Francisco District Attorney Chesa Boudin was recalled by his entirely Democrat, far-left voting base due to his perceived negligence.[cliii] With a whopping sixty percent voting to recall him, San Francisco's voters rejected Boudin's hard-left policies such as ending cash bail, stopping the prosecution of minors as adults, and lowering jail populations amid the Covid-19 pandemic. Boudin was also the first San Francisco DA to file homicide charges against city police officers.

Momentum to recall Boudin picked up steam throughout 2021 as hate crimes against Asian Americans in San Francisco increased dramatically and victims blamed Boudin, saying he was siding with criminals. Recall supporters also pointed to car break-ins and viral smash-and-grab robberies at major retail stores, claiming they were becoming common occurrences as consequences of Boudin's policies.[cliv]

Does this mean San Francisco has suddenly become a right-leaning city? Of course not. Mary Jung, the chair of the recall effort against

Boudin had this to say: "This election does not mean that San Francisco has drifted to the far right on our approach to criminal justice. In fact, San Francisco has been a national beacon for progressive criminal justice reform for decades and will continue to do so with new leadership."

Media pundits have offered solutions for helping minority-majority neighborhoods as a strictly binary choice: vote Republican and have low crime at the expense of civil liberties, or vote Democrat and accept high crime as the cost of your freedom. It is not, and has never been, a binary choice.

Social programs, to the exclusion of all else, do not keep communities safe or prosperous and the voters of San Francisco had had enough. Likewise, heavy-handed law enforcement without accountability eats away at community cohesion and prosperity. You do not have to choose one over the other. This is why local elections are important. It isn't the president or your senator who tends to your city's criminal justice system, your infrastructure, or funding for social programs. It's your governor (elected official), district attorney (elected official), your mayor (elected official), and your police chief (appointed by the mayor). Do not sit out local elections because they make the news less. They are vitally important to your standard of living and the level of safety in your community.

What combination of law enforcement and social programs you most prefer is highly individual and, in some cases, may only be solved by moving to another city or even to another state. During the Covid-19 lockdowns, many people were given the push they needed to leave their hometowns for something more in line with their values, bringing their vote with them.

Remember, it's not just your vote that matters. Your property taxes and state income tax (if applicable) pay for schools, police, and local business loans for minority-owned businesses. Where you choose to live has power, maybe even more than your vote. Remember that.

CHAPTER 17
RURAL AMERICA CHALLENGES
★★★★★

"A bright future for the nation depends on the health and prosperity of rural America."
—Kristen Gillibrand

Rural communities often get short shrift when it comes to news coverage and attention to the issues they face. Because crime and other attention-grabbing disasters are rare in rural communities as compared to urban areas, many policymakers and the majority of the American public give little thought to the people who live in small, remote towns. Living in a rural community is much more than the pastoral stock footage of fields, cows, and stunning sunsets. Regardless of which state you live in, tending to the needs of rural communities is vital. These are the communities that grow and raise our food. They are where food processing plants are located. In some cases, they are also where our factories, arms silos, and toxic waste disposal sites are located. Never underestimate the importance of rural America. Leaving them unattended or underfunded can have disastrous implications for our broader society.

Dying Rural Towns
Most imagine rural America to be driven largely by the agriculture, manufacturing, and mining industries. While there are other industries in rural communities (retail for instance), these three are the main

drivers of rural prosperity. In our modern, globalized economy, one of those drivers (manufacturing) has all but collapsed, devastating many rural communities.

Additionally, rural communities that are involved in mining can have their economies swing wildly depending upon who is currently president and who has control of Congress. This is because Republican policies tend to prioritize domestic energy (oil, coal, and fracking) production and manufacturing while Democrat policies tend to result in a reduction of domestic energy production and manufacturing. As we have discussed, domestic energy production and manufacturing creates jobs and reduces our reliance on foreign actors. On the other hand, reducing domestic energy production and manufacturing arguably helps achieve targeted climate-related goals. It is beyond the scope of this book to argue for or against either approach. However, it is important that voters understand the implications of various policy decisions.

Rural areas constitute ninety-seven percent of America's land mass. Yet, our policymakers, at least at the federal level, tend to be from urban or suburban backgrounds and legislate accordingly. In some cases, lawmakers have been openly disdainful of rural communities and naively wonder why their voices should matter at all.[clv]

Despite the importance of rural communities to the overall strength of our nation, federal policy often overlooks rural communities leaving them to struggle with poverty in many cases. Beyond dealing with a lack of jobs and economic opportunities for growth, some rural areas also struggle with accessing important services like health care and even reliable internet service.

Ironically, food availability is consistently a problem for many rural communities, even though they overwhelmingly are the ones producing food for the rest of us.

- *Paradoxically, in rural areas that grow most of our nation's food, households face considerably deeper struggles with hunger than those in metropolitan areas.*

- *12.1% of rural households faced food insecurity in 2020, compared to 10.3% of households in metropolitan areas.*

- *Food insecurity is linked to a wide range of negative health outcomes, and rural Americans are at higher risk for poor health outcomes than their urban counterparts.*

- *SNAP [Supplemental Nutrition Assistance Program] participation nationally was highest among households in rural (16 percent) and small town (15 percent) counties compared to households in metro counties (13 percent) (American Community Survey 2016 five-year estimates – 2012–2016).*

- *Rural residents who are eligible for SNAP often miss out on benefits because they lack information and disproportionately lack access to apply and recertify for benefits.[clvi]*

The Targeted Destruction of the Independent Family Farm

"I love farming and have been doing it all my life, but I told my kids not to come back to the farm, because there's no future in it. That's the sad truth." These are the words of Darvin Bentlage, a fourth-generation cattle and grain farmer from Missouri. In June of 2022, he told his story to the Missouri Independent[clvii] and his experience as a family farmer is reflective of a greater, long-term problem with America's farms.

Over the last three decades, roughly 40% of U.S. family cattle operations have gone out of business. Over those same three decades, the U.S. had a 25% reduction in cattle farmers as a whole and a whopping 90% of U.S. hog farmers were put out of business. It doesn't take a social scientist to understand why the average age of a farmer is nearing sixty years old. The younger generation doesn't see the benefit.

Why is this happening? Corporations (some American, some not) now control much of the American farming enterprise and have used their size and scale to influence politicians in both parties.

Opponents of the corporate model of farming—based on the unanimous assessment of both right-leaning farmers and left-leaning environmental activists—contend that it is bad for consumers (additives and pesticides in our food), bad for rural economies (no jobs), bad for our environment and our climate (factory farms work against the landscape and animal biology instead of with it), and bad for democracy. So many of the laws and regulations regarding farming have been written by corporate lobbyists and introduced by overly accommodating legislators.

The U.S. imports billions of pounds of beef from around the world, and consumers are paying record high prices, all while American cattle farmers are being put out of business. Even if the package you buy at the store says US beef, that doesn't mean the cows were raised or slaughtered here. It just means the beef was processed here. In 2021, the U.S. imported 3.35 billion pounds of beef and 1.8 million live cattle.[clviii]

Corporate agriculture is incredibly lucrative and they use it to their advantage in the halls of Congress, where family farmers have little to no influence. A bit of perspective may be helpful.

> In 2021,…a Brazilian corporation and the world's biggest meatpacker net revenue was $71 billion and their U.S. beef division reported a net revenue of $27.18 billion; [a U.S. competitor - company A] had a net profit of $3.05 billion, up $1 billion from 2020; [U.S. company B] reported its biggest profit in its 156-year history, netting almost $5 billion; …the Chinese corporation that owns [U.S. company B], reported $27.29 billion in revenue, up 6.7%.[clix]

The market for produce is no better than the realities of livestock. If anything, it might be worse. There are several large-scale producers that exert a tremendous amount of pressure and influence on the marketplace and their actions may sometimes be at odds with or even detrimental to small-scale producers and even consumers. Public media sources have highlighted the interest of corporate agriculture juxtaposed against the interests of rural farmers.

For example, a massive conglomerate has been accused of intentionally selling pesticides which are strongly linked to cancer.[clx] They have also developed a reputation for suing farmers, forcing them to either settle out of court or fight the lawsuit and potentially face financial ruin. What are these lawsuits about? The conglomerate patents their seeds (which is a hotly debated topic beyond the scope of this book). That means the farmers who purchase the conglomerate's seeds cannot use them again next year. Instead of using their existing wheat crop, for instance, to harvest seeds for the next season, they must purchase new ones. Every year, the company changes its formula slightly, files a new patent, and checks to make sure farms aren't reusing seeds. And suing them into bankruptcy if they do.

For some farmers, [the Company's] investigation of them will lead to the courtroom. To date, [the Company] has filed 90 lawsuits against American farmers.

The lawsuits involve 147 farmers and 39 small businesses or farm companies, and have been directed at farmers residing in half of the states in the U.S. The odds are clearly stacked against the farmer: [The Company] has an annual budget of $10 million dollars and a staff of 75 devoted solely to investigating and prosecuting farmers.[clxi]

Even farmers who do not use the conglomerate's seeds can get sued. For example, a Canadian farmer was sued by the company for misappropriating patented property. The company claimed the farmer was using genetically modified canola seed without a license. However, the farmer maintained he used seeds purchased elsewhere and that the seed had drifted onto his property from neighboring farms. Though he proffered evidence that the contamination did not benefit his annual output and thus earnings at all, he still lost his case.

Why is this kind of targeted destruction of American industry by corporations permitted? Because our leaders (who again, mostly are not from rural communities and may have never even visited one) have allowed it. Though Republican leaders tend to use rural imagery in their campaign videos and appeal to rural voters in their talking points, their actions in terms of resisting agro-business lobbies and legislation are often no better[clxii] than their Democrat colleagues, who generally focus on urban concerns.

The state of rural America is everyone's problem, no matter where we live. The availability and nutritional quality of the food we consume effects the health of our nation. It effects our medical costs and the quality of care we receive. It effects the prices we pay for food. It effects the care we give to the animals we use for food. And yes, it effects our planet.

Billion-dollar multinational corporations were not elected to serve us and they do not answer to us. Your representatives do. If you are a city or suburb dweller, it may not rank high on your list of concerns. But when electing a national-level candidate, I heartily recommend you look into the candidate's plans for farmers, their support of the USDA. Even examining their opinions on lowering the expensive barrier to entry for having food certified as organic.

Our food, fuel, and manufacturing are critically important to the health and welfare of our country. Rural America not only plays a vital role in delivering those capabilities, but its success is also essential for our nation's continued strength. If we neglect rural America, we do so at our own peril.

CHAPTER 18
HOMELESSNESS

"Homelessness…is neither a disease nor crime…
but a very serious problem!"
—Timothy Pina

No matter where you live or how you vote, you have likely seen homeless people in your town or city. Unfortunately, homelessness exists in every society, though a high concentration of unhoused people in a city or state can be indicative of larger problems. The great majority of homeless people are only unhoused temporarily, thanks to the system of temporary and long-term shelters in each state. People who lose their home because they lost their job or lack sufficient financial resources are often able to eventually find new opportunities and resources to remedy their situation.

However, there are chronically homeless people—those who live on the streets not simply because they've had a bout of bad luck. These are people afflicted with mental illness, people who suffer from addiction, or simply those whose lives are seemingly so unbearable that they have developed antisocial traits, making it difficult for them to cope with society. Homeless Americans are every bit as diverse as the rest of the country and all of them need help. It is incumbent upon us to understand that their needs may differ based on their unique circumstances.

Who are the Homeless?

Men and boys are the most populous group among the homeless, with 22 out of every 10,000 males being homeless. By contrast, 13 out of every 10,000 are women or girls. Most women and girls who experience homelessness are a part of a family unit, which are treated differently and given higher priority than individual homeless people.[clxiii]

Race is another significant predictor. Because white people (at least for now) are the majority in the U.S., it is reasonable and expected that white men are the largest racial group among the homeless, accounting for more than a quarter-million people. However, African Americans and other marginalized groups are more likely to be disadvantaged with regard to unemployment rates, lower incomes, less access to healthcare, and higher incarceration rates, making them far more likely to experience homelessness in their lifetime.

Within non-white populations, Native Hawaiians and other Pacific Islanders have the highest rate of homelessness (109 out of every 10,000 people). Native Americans (45 out of every 10,000) and Black or African Americans (52 out of every 10,000) also experience elevated rates.

Military Veteran Homelessness

Like family units, veterans are another group of homeless people that are analyzed and processed differently within the homeless system. Due to their service to our country, and the understandably high rate of PTSD and other trauma responses, unhoused veterans have resources available especially for them. It is a tribute to the Department of Veterans Affairs as well as state agencies that as of 2020, veterans are only six percent of people experiencing homelessness. Six percent is still too many, but it represents an improvement from times past. Given how many of our men and women fought in Afghanistan and Iraq during the twenty years of conflict, it seems the Veterans Administration and our healthcare establishment have learned lessons from the Vietnam era and made some course corrections.

In fact, eighty-two communities and three states have announced that they have ended veterans' homelessness entirely. This means their systems can ensure that homelessness is rare, brief, and one-time for military veterans. Nationally, veteran homelessness has decreased thirty-nine percent since 2007.

Thankfully, veterans are not the only groups to have benefited from more robust shelter systems and other aid programs. Unhoused families with children have decreased by twenty-seven percent since 2007.

On the other hand, chronic individual homelessness *had* dropped by thirty-five percent from 2007 to 2016. But then it shot up higher than ever, with a seventy percent increase from 2016 to 2020. There is no one single cause to point to that would explain this rise. Maybe it is an increase in drug use. Or maybe it's a sign that more individuals feel alienated from our broader society and choose to drop out of it. It is difficult to say and it is probably a complicated web of reasons. Nonetheless, homeless Americans need help, and not just from benevolent individuals and charitable nonprofits that do great work in our cities and towns. They can help plug the leak, but our legislators need to develop effective policies to mitigate the risk of homelessness.

Republican Views on Homelessness

Generally, the major difference between Democrat and Republican lawmakers is the use of public space. Do unhoused people have the right to sleep on the street? In parks? Under bridges? If so, can they set up a tent? Can they panhandle and during what times? Republican governors and mayors are traditionally more inclined to say no to all of this.

Not only does the presence of homeless people discourage commerce, they say, it is also deeply unkind to the homeless people themselves. The Daily Wire's Michael Knowles has said of the proliferation of tent cities in places like LA:

I know there is the feeling that we should be as nice as we can to people, that we should be compassionate, but they need to go get help... They should try to get their lives back on track. If they need mental health help, they should be brought to places where there is mental health help. If they're criminals, they should go to prison. The one place they shouldn't go is a tent on the street.[clxiv]

There are anti-camping ordnances in many cities to prevent this sort of visible homelessness. Likewise, there are laws against panhandling (in general or in certain locations). Republican-led cities are also more likely to empower police to issue trespass warnings on their own, instead of requiring the property owner to request one. These policies are not designed to punish people for being homeless, but rather to direct them to shelters or, if needed, to hospitals or mental health treatment.

Democrat Views on Homelessness

San Francisco has become a case study of sorts for Democrat policies on homelessness. And, when looking at a map of homelessness rates in our country, an interesting observation emerges. The highest concentrations of homelessness are largely found in Democrat-run states.

However, the high incidence of homelessness in those states is not necessarily due to the Democrat platform in and of itself. Instead, it is likely more appropriately attributed to policy failures in those states over a lengthy period and the personal ideologies of their politicians. Elsewhere throughout the country, most states have rates of homelessness that are somewhat comparable. California, Washington, Oregon, and New York may have the worst rates in the country, but solidly Democrat states like Illinois and purple states like Virginia are no better or worse than Republican-led Kansas.

The Democrats believe in freedom of movement and the right to be unhoused; this is a part of their platform. Policy critics contend that what is unique to the hard-left policies of California (San Francisco in particular) and Washington (particularly Seattle) is that the unhoused are often given preference over others, at the expense of cleanliness, order, and safety.

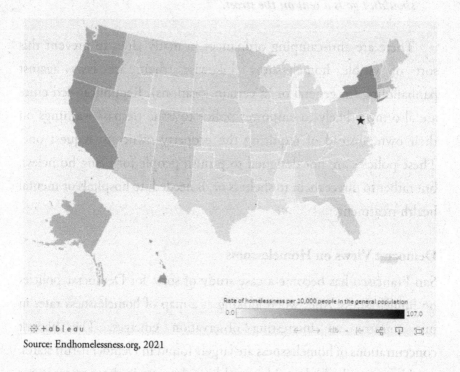

Rate of homelessness per 10,000 people in the general population
0.0 — 107.0

⊕ + tableau

Source: Endhomelessness.org, 2021

The policies in the dark blue states, however, do not appear to be in line with most Democrat lawmakers, nor Democrat voters. In fact, the residents of Seattle, who can be assumed to be overwhelmingly Democrat voters, have started to take matters into their own hands to combat homelessness:

Business and property owners in Seattle are installing 1-ton concrete blocks on city streets to prevent RVs and homeless encampments from forming or returning to an area.

"Individual businesses and residents are putting ecology blocks out as taking matters in their own hands because if they call the city and say there are RVs out in front of their business or out in front of their home, they can't do anything about it," [a] business owner told The Seattle Times.

Anonymous Seattleites have hauled the massive 1 to 2-ton blocks – known as "ecology blocks" or "eco blocks" – using special equipment outside residential areas and in front of businesses to prevent RVs from parking and homeless encampments from forming.[clxv]

In passing laws that permit homeless communities to develop in front of homes and businesses, against the wishes of residents and customers, the tax-paying citizens of Seattle are starting to believe that their concerns don't matter. Give the government your (extremely high) taxes and put up with it. Most other Democrat-led states do not do this, so it is unfair to ascribe this philosophy to the entire Democrat party.

Generally, Democrats fund rehabilitation initiatives while allowing unhoused people to remain unhoused if they so wish. Though most cities have curfews for panhandling—places where panhandling is always forbidden and laws regarding public intoxication or lewdness, which are enforced by the police. These policies are generally acceptable to people in both parties

Outcome-Based Solutions

Most municipalities use something called a Continuum of Care (CoC) when it comes to directing homeless people to the correct services. According to the U.S. Department of Housing and Urban Development (HUD), a CoC is "a community plan to organize and deliver housing and services to meet the specific needs of people who are homeless as they move to stable housing and maximize self-sufficiency. It includes action steps to end homelessness and prevent a return to homelessness." HUD identifies four necessary parts of a continuum:

- *Outreach, intake, and assessment in order to identify service and housing needs and provide a link to the appropriate level of both;*
- *Emergency shelter to provide an immediate and safe alternative to sleeping on the streets, especially for homeless families with children;*
- *Transitional housing with supportive services to allow for the development of skills that will be needed once permanently housed; and*
- *Permanent and permanent supportive housing to provide individuals and families with an affordable place to live with services if needed.*[clxvi]

Both parties acknowledge that having a CoC is the right choice. The only point of disagreement is which step should come first. Republicans tend to favor a services-first model, while Democrats tend to favor a housing-first model, which has two major tenets: (1) the most effective solution to homelessness is permanent housing; and (2) all housing for the homeless should be provided immediately, without any preconditions, such as sobriety requirements.

California operates on a housing first model, which is well-intentioned, but the results show that it has not worked.

- *Housing First has not been shown to be effective in ending homelessness at the community level, but rather, only for individuals.*
- *A Housing First intervention for a small segment of "high*

utilizer" homeless people may save taxpayers money. But making Housing First the organizing principle of homeless services systems, as urged by many advocates, will not save taxpayers money.

- *Housing is not the same as treatment. Housing First's record at addressing behavioral health disorders, such as untreated serious mental illness and drug addiction, is far weaker than its record at promoting residential stability.*

- *Housing First's record at promoting employment and addressing social isolation for the homeless is also weaker than its record at promoting residential stability.*[clxvii]

People are homeless for many reasons, but addiction and mental illness are near the top of the list. Without addressing those problems first, any provision of housing seems unlikely to be helpful in the long term. Salt Lake City found that out firsthand when they implemented their housing-first initiative, touting to the world that they had effectively ended homelessness in their city. Except…they didn't. Not even close. Allegedly, they just fudged the numbers, changing who they counted as homeless, and now in 2022, homelessness in Salt Lake City is believed to be worse than ever.[clxviii]

In 2020, The Manhattan Institute released a report stating that the housing-first initiative is not effective on a large scale and that HUD should allow more flexibility.[clxix] Allowing localities to choose their own solutions in line with the local electorate's wishes is the key to successfully reducing homelessness while protecting the rest of the citizenry.

The plight of homeless Americans is one that deserves care and consideration. We must not turn a blind eye to the problem. And when crafting solutions, we cannot ignore the resulting impact to the rest of the population. This is something both parties can agree on.

CONCLUSION

Above all things, I hope this book has given you the tools to ask yourself and your elected officials probing questions about the issues that matter most to you. To vote our way into the country we want to live in, we first need to be aware of what the issues are and where the two major parties generally stand on them. In this book, you have read about different issues—some of which you have heard about in the news, perhaps extensively. Some others, you may not have been aware of at all.

Though our officials are indeed elected to speak for us, to pursue our best interests, and to fight for the weakest among us, I think we can agree that doesn't always happen. Maybe it feels like it never happens. The way to ensure it does is to vote, to speak at public meetings, and to research candidates and issues before election day. Sometimes it can feel overwhelming and most of us have quite enough on our plate without doing extra work to make sure our concerns are being addressed by our legislators.

As I said in the first chapter, my goal is not to persuade you to vote one way or another…or to prefer one party over another. Our country has incredible diversity, both in our physical characteristics and in our diversity of thought. This diversity is our strength, but only if we use it to make educated decisions with a specific goal in mind.

What that goal is remains for you, the voting public, to decide. Whatever it is, I hope *People Over Politics* helps you become more informed about the important issues impacting our country. And I hope it helps you identify and select the candidates best equipped to lead our country and to create the society you wish to see. In the end, I hope you are inspired to push your legislators to put people over politics!

REFERENCES

★★★★★

[i] Haidt, J. (2015). Why working-class people vote conservative. *The Guardian*. https://www.theguardian.com/society/2012/jun/05/why-working-class-people-vote-conservative

[ii] Hart, K. (2018). Exclusive poll: Most Democrats see Republicans as racist, sexist. *Axios*. https://www.axios.com/poll-democrats-and-republicans-hate-each-other-racist-ignorant-evil-99ae7afc-5a51-42be-8ee2-3959e43ce320.html

[iii] Locke, J. (1690). Second Treatise on Government. *The Gutenberg Institute*. https://www.gutenberg.org/files/7370/7370-h/7370-h.htm

[iv] Madison, J. (1788). Federalist Papers No. 51. *The Bill of Rights Institute*. https://billofrightsinstitute.org/primary-sources/federalist-no-51

[v] Jones, N.H. (2019). The 1619 Project. *The New York Times*. https://www.nytimes.com/interactive/2019/08/14/magazine/1619-america-slavery.html

[vi] Ellis, R. (2020). George Washington statue toppled in Portland. *OPB News*. https://www.opb.org/news/article/george-washington-statue-toppled-portland/

[vii] Sharp, J. (2021). Statue of US President Thomas Jefferson removed from New York City Hall over slavery links. *Sky News*. https://news.sky.com/story/statue-of-us-president-thomas-jefferson-removed-from-new-york-city-hall-over-slavery-links-12476201

[viii] Op-Ed: We The People Should Throw Out The Constitution (2013). Talk of the Nation. *NPR*. https://www.npr.org/2013/01/03/168549290/the-constitution-just-a-poetic-piece-of-parchment

[ix] The Daily Wire (2017). Shapiro Deconstructs The Myth 'America Was Founded On Slavery' In New Video. https://www.dailywire.com/news/watch-shapiro-deconstructs-myth-america-was-daily-wire

^x Pruitt, S. (2019). The Founding Fathers Feared Political Factions Would Tear the Nation Apart. *History Stories.* https://www.history.com/news/founding-fathers-political-parties-opinion

^{xi} The Republican National Committee (2016). Our Platform. *GOP.com.* https://gop.com/about-our-party/

^{xii} Desilver, D. (2019). Clinton's impeachment barely dented his public support, and it turned off many Americans. *Pew Research Center.* https://www.pewresearch.org/fact-tank/2019/10/03/clintons-impeachment-barely-dented-his-public-support-and-it-turned-off-many-americans/

^{xiii} Murphy, M.E. (2020). African Americans in the Great Depression and New Deal. *The Oxford Research Encyclopedia, American History.* https://doi.org/10.1093/acrefore/9780199329175.013.632

^{xiv} Kessler, R. (1995). *Inside the White House: The Hidden Lives of the Modern Presidents and the Secrets of the World's Most Powerful Institution.* New York: Simon & Schuster

^{xv} X, Malcolm (1964). The ballot or the bullet. *EdChange.org.* http://www.edchange.org/multicultural/speeches/malcolm_x_ballot.html

^{xvi} Mellowes, Marilyn. God in America – The Black Church. https://www.pbs.org/wgbh/americanexperience/features/godinamerica-black-church/

^{xvii} Reyes, R. (2021). Why noncitizens should be allowed to vote. *CNN.* https://www.cnn.com/2021/12/10/opinions/new-york-city-noncitizen-voting-smart-policy-reyes/index.html

^{xviii} Associated Press (2021). N.C. Judges Strike Down A Voter ID Law They Say Discriminates Against Black Voters. *NPR.* https://www.npr.org/2021/09/17/1038354159/n-c-judges-strike-down-a-voter-id-law-they-say-discriminates-against-black-voter

^{xix} Fox News (2016). *Ami Horowitz: How white liberals really view black voters.* https://www.youtube.com/watch?v=yW2LpFkVfYk

^{xx} Dunn, A. (2020). *Fact check: Over 159 million people voted in the US general election. USA Today.*

https://www.usatoday.com/story/news/factcheck/2020/12/30/fact-check-fals-president-than-were-registered-u-s/4010087001/

xxi The Legislative Branch (2022). *Whitehouse.gov.* https://www.whitehouse.gov/about-the-white-house/our-government/the-legislative-branch/

xxii Saad, L. (2013). Americans Call for Term Limits, End to Electoral College. *Gallup.* https://news.gallup.com/poll/159881/americans-call-term-limits-end-electoral-college.aspx

xxiii Soffen, K. (2016). *How racial gerrymandering deprives black people of political power. Washington Post.* https://www.washingtonpost.com/news/wonk/wp/2016/06/09/how-a-widespread-practice-to-politically-empower-african americans-might-actually-harm-them/

xxiv Brennan Center for Justice (2022). Redistricting Litigation Roundup. https://www.brennancenter.org/our-work/research-reports/redistricting-litigation-roundup-0

xxv Dickerson, J. (2016). Changes to the role of the presidency. *The Khan Academy.* https://www.khanacademy.org/humanities/us-government-and-civics/us-gov-interactions-among-branches/us-gov-expansion-of-presidential-power/v/changes-to-the-role-of-the-presidency

xxvi Ibid.

xxvii Ballard, Jamie (2020). What leadership qualities do Americans want in a president? https://today.yougov.com/topics/politics/articles-reports/2020/08/06/leadership-qualities-president-poll-data

xxviii Public Trust in Government: 1958-2021 (2021). *Pew Research.* https://www.pewresearch.org/politics/2021/05/17/public-trust-in-government-1958-2021/

xxix Britannica (2022). *Supreme Court of the United States.* https://www.britannica.com/topic/Supreme-Court-of-the-United-States/Procedures-and-power

xxx Williams, C. (2021). Why exactly does the U.S. Supreme Court have 9 Justices? *KSL.* https://www.ksl.com/article/50156678/why-exactly-does-the-us-supreme-court-have-9-justices

xxxi LawyerEdu (2021). *Top 10 most controversial U.S. Supreme Court Cases.*
https://www.lawyeredu.org/most-controversial-court-cases.html

xxxii Bruenig, M. (2020). What exactly is the liberal position on the Supreme Court? *People's Policy Project.*
peoplespolicyproject.org/2020/09/20/what-exactly-is-the-liberal-position-on-the-supreme-court/

xxxiii Callahan, M. (2018). Why do supreme court justices have lifetime appointments? *News@Northeastern.*
https://news.northeastern.edu/2018/09/21/why-do-supreme-court-justices-have-lifetime-appointments/

xxxiv U.S. Life expectancy 1950-2022. *Macrotrends.*
https://www.macrotrends.net/countries/U.S.A/united-states/life-expectancy

xxxv Davidson, P. (2019). Millennials, Gen Xers to baby boomers: Can you retire so I can get a job promotion? *U.S.A Today.*
https://www.usatoday.com/story/money/2019/11/07/jobs-baby-boomers-older-workers-may-block-millennials-careers/4170836002/

xxxvi Roberts, R. (2021). This Senate is the oldest in American history. Should we do anything about it? *The Washington Post.*
https://www.washingtonpost.com/lifestyle/2021/06/02/senate-age-term-limits/

xxxvii Viser, M. et al. (2022). Inside the campaign to pressure Justice Stephen Breyer to retire. *Washington Post.*
https://www.washingtonpost.com/politics/2022/01/29/inside-campaign-pressure-justice-stephen-breyer-retire/

xxxviii Elkind, E. (2022). SCOTU.S. Justice Breyer was 'blindsided' by announcement he was retiring after Biden's Chief of Staff Ron Klain leaked news to a 'limited number' of Dems - less than TWO HOURS before it was made public. *Daily Mail.*
https://www.dailymail.co.uk/news/article-10464283/Bidens-Chief-Staff-Ron-Klain-revealed-Breyers-retirement-limited-group-leaked.html

xxxix Social Security Administration (2022). *Historical Background and development of Social Security.*

https://www.ssa.gov/history/briefhistory3.html

xl Paul, T. (2022). Will Social Security run out of money? Here's what could happen to your benefits if Congress does not act. *CNBC*. https://www.cnbc.com/select/will-social-security-run-out-heres-what-you-need-to-know

xli Ibid.

xlii United States Census Bureau (2017). *Who are the uninsured?* https://www.census.gov/newsroom/blogs/random-samplings/2017/09/who_are_the_uninsure.html

xliii Von Drehle, D. (2017). The real reason health care in America is a mess. *The Washington Post.* https://www.washingtonpost.com/opinions/the-real-reason-health-care-in-america-is-a-mess/2017/09/23/28e8f7cc-9f97-11e7-8ea1-ed975285475e_story.html?noredirect=on&utm_term=.2c295ae9fe2d

xliv Kotecha, S. (2010). How does U.S. healthcare work? *BBC News.* http://www.bbc.co.uk/newsbeat/article/10067521/how-does-us-healthcare-work

xlv Yang, J. (2022). Affordable Care Act – Statistics and Facts. *Statista.* https://www.statista.com/topics/3272/obamacare/#dossierKeyfigures

xlvi Keith, K. (2021). Supreme Court rejects ACA challenge. *Health Affairs.* https://www.healthaffairs.org/do/10.1377/forefront.20210617.665248/full/

xlvii Walsh, M. (2018). There is no way to justify the murder of Alfie Evans. *Daily Wire.* https://www.dailywire.com/news/walsh-doctors-and-judges-will-murder-alfie-evans-matt-walsh

xlviii Dalen, J. et al. (2015). Why do so many Americans oppose the Affordable Care Act? *PubMed.* https://pubmed.ncbi.nlm.nih.gov/25731135/#:~:text=Despite%20these%20positive%20changes%2C%20a,government%20role%20in%20health%20care.

xlix Noonan et al. (2016). Improving the health of African Americans in the U.S.: An overdue opportunity for social justice. *Public Health Review, 37*(12). doi: 10.1186/s40985-016-0025-4

[i] Peter G. Peterson Foundation (2021). *Income and wealth in the United States: An overview of recent data.* pgpf.org/blog/2021/11/income-and-wealth-in-the-united-states-an-overview-of-data

[ii] Taylor, J. (2019). Racism, Inequality, and Health Care for African Americans. *The Century Foundation.* https://tcf.org/content/report/racism-inequality-health-care-African Americans/

[iii] Noonan et al. (2016).

[iv] Pfizer (n.d.). Health disparities among African Americans. https://www.pfizer.com/news/articles/health_disparities_among_african _americans

[v] Johnson, B. (2021). How the Virginia governor's race was won. *Daily Wire.* https://www.dailywire.com/news/how-the-virginia-governors-race-was-won

[vi] Burke, L. (2021). The Education Lesson from COVID Lockdowns: School Choice Is Imperative for Every Child. *Daily Wire.* https://www.dailywire.com/news/the-education-lesson-from-covid-lockdowns-school-choice-is-imperative-for-every-child

[vii] Waraich, S. (2022). The pandemic strained Humboldt County students' academics. *The Eureka Times-Standard.* https://www.times-standard.com/2022/03/19/the-pandemic-strained-humboldt-county-students-academics/

[viii] Burke, L. (2021).

[ix] https://www.theroot.com/blacks-and-education-what-we-learn-1790878682

[x] https://datacenter.kidscount.org/data/tables/10120-high-school-graduation-rates-by-race-and-ethnicity

[xi] Garcia, E. (2020). Schools are still segregated, and black children are paying a price. *Economic Policy Institute.* https://www.epi.org/publication/schools-are-still-segregated-and-black-children-are-paying-a-price/

[xii] Ibid.

[xiii] ASCE (2021). Report card for America's Infrastructure.

https://infrastructurereportcard.org/making-the-grade/

lxiii Johnson, B. (2021). Where Does All That Money Go? Breaking Down Biden's Trillion Dollar Infrastructure Package. *Daily Wire.* https://www.dailywire.com/news/where-does-all-that-money-go-breaking-down-bidens-trillion-dollar-infrastructure-package

lxiv Technometrica Market Intelligence (2015). *High-Speed Rail in America.* https://www.apta.com/wp-content/uploads/Resources/resources/reports andpublications/Documents/APTA-2015-High-Speed-Train-Survey.pdf

lxv Murdock, D. (2022). Biden blames Putin for high gas prices — but this timeline proves it is the prez's own fault. *NY Post.* https://nypost.com/2022/03/18/president-biden-is-at-fault-for-high-gas-prices-not-putin/

lxvi OPEC (2022). Member countries. *About Us.* https://www.opec.org/opec_web/en/about_us/25.htm

lxvii Reed, S. (2020). How a Saudi-Russian Standoff Sent Oil Markets in a Frenzy. *New York Times.* https://www.nytimes.com/2020/03/09/business/energy-environment/oil-opec-saudi-russia.html

lxviii Schukman, D. (2022). What is fracking and why is it controversial? *BBC.* https://www.bbc.com/news/uk-14432401

lxix Dews, F. (2015). *The economic benefits of fracking.* Brookings. https://www.brookings.edu/blog/brookings-now/2015/03/23/the-economic-benefits-of-fracking/

lxx U.S.GS (2022). Does fracking cause earthquakes? https://www.usgs.gov/faqs/does-fracking-cause-earthquakes

lxxi Roberts, D. (2018). How to save the failing nuclear power plants that generate half of America's clean electricity. *Vox.* https://www.vox.com/energy-and-environment/2018/5/10/17334474/nuclear-power-renewables-plants-retirements-us

lxxii Shane, L. (2021). Trust in the military is dropping significantly, new survey suggests. Military Times. https://www.militarytimes.com/news/pentagon-congress/2021/03/10/trust-in-the-military-is-dropping-significantly-new-survey-suggests/

lxxiii Britannica (2022). *U.S. Department of Defense.*
https://www.britannica.com/topic/U.S.-Department-of-Defense

lxxiv DeSimone, D. (2022). 6 Moments of Bravery in African American
Military History. *U.S.O.* https://www.uso.org/stories/2308-bravery-in-
African American-military-history

lxxv History (2021). The Tuskegee Airmen.
https://www.history.com/topics/world-war-ii/tuskegee-airmen

lxxvi Nalty, B. (n.d.). The Right to Fight: African American Marines in
World War II. *National Parks Service.*
https://www.nps.gov/parkhistory/online_books/npswapa/extcontent/us
mc/pcn-190-003132-00/sec1.htm

lxxvii Bamford, T. (2020). African Americans Fought for Freedom at Home
and Abroad during World War II. *The National WWII Museum.*
https://www.nationalww2museum.org/war/articles/African Americans-
fought-freedom-home-and-abroad-during-world-war-ii

lxxviii Black Past (n.d.). The Commanders: Admirals And Generals In The
United States Military, 1940–. https://www.blackpast.org/special-
features/the-commanders-admirals-and-generals/

lxxix Morris, T. (2017). Obama's 'red line' failure assured crisis in Syria.
NOLO. https://www.nola.com/opinions/article_3635bdcb-4a9f-595a-
a34f-35863ecdc303.html

lxxx Berlinski, C. (2018). Europe's dependence on the U.S. was all part of the
plan. Politico. https://www.politico.eu/article/europe-dependence-on-
the-us-was-all-part-of-the-plan-donald-trump-nato/

lxxxi Schuman, M. (2020). What Happens When China Leads the World?
The Atlantic. https://www.theatlantic.com/international/archive/
2020/10/what-kind-superpower-will-china-be/616580/

lxxxii Cohn, D. (2015). How U.S. immigration laws and rules have changed
through history. *Pew Research Center.*
https://www.pewresearch.org/fact-tank/2015/09/30/how-u-s-
immigration-laws-and-rules-have-changed-through-history/

lxxxiii Ibid.

lxxxiv U.S. House of Representatives (2022). Immigration and Nationality

Act of 1965. *History, Art, and Archives.*
https://history.house.gov/Historical-Highlights/1951-
2000/Immigration-and-Nationality-Act-of-1965/

lxxxv Cohn, D. (2015).

lxxxvi Beck, R. (1996). The Case Against Immigration. *The Washington Post.*
https://www.washingtonpost.com/wp-srv/style/longterm/books/
chap1/againsti.htm

lxxxvii Tekelova, M. (2011). A debt based monetary system, export warfare &
third world debt. *Positive Money.* https://positivemoney.org/2011/12/
debt-based-monetary-system-world-debt/

lxxxviii Loren Siegel Consulting (2010). Bridging the Black-Immigrant Divide.
The Opportunity Agenda. https://www.opportunityagenda.org/explore/
resources-publications/bridging-black-immigrant-divide

lxxxix Marx, W. (2022). Britain has partnered with Rwanda to process and
settle thousands of migrants. *NPR.*
https://www.npr.org/2022/04/18/1093380846/britain-has-partnered-
with-rwanda-to-process-and-settle-thousands-of-migrants

xc Adkins, T. (2022). What the national debt means to you. *Investopedia.*
https://www.investopedia.com/articles/economics/10/national-debt.asp

xci Ibid.

xcii O'Neill says Cheney told him 'Deficits don't matter.' (2004). *Chicago
Tribune.* https://www.chicagotribune.com/news/ct-xpm-2004-01-12-
0401120168-story.html

xciii Fontinelle, A. (2022). A brief history of taxes in the U.S. *Investopedia.*
https://www.investopedia.com/articles/tax/10/history-taxes.asp

xciv Ibid.

xcv 2021 Tax brackets and federal income tax rates. *TurboTax.*
https://turbotax.intuit.com/tax-tools/calculators/tax-bracket/

xcvi Who pays income taxes? *National Taxpayers Union Foundation.*
https://www.ntu.org/foundation/tax-page/who-pays-income-taxes

xcvii Zeisloft, B. (2021). Democrats appear to back down from 'unrealized
capital gains' tax. *Daily Wire.* https://www.dailywire.com/news/
democrats-appear-to-back-down-from-unrealized-capital-gains-tax

xcviii Massaglia, A. (2022). Intuit spends millions lobbying amid accusations of deceptive TurboTax advertising. *Open Secrets.* https://www.opensecrets.org/news/2022/03/intuit-spends-millions-lobbying-amid-accusations-of-deceptive-turbotax-advertising/

xcix Ibid.

c BBC. (2017). *What is the Republican tax plan?* https://www.bbc.com/news/business-42375212

ci Watson, G. (2022). Proposed Minimum Tax on Billionaire Capital Gains Takes Tax Code in Wrong Direction. Tax Foundation. https://taxfoundation.org/biden-billionaire-tax-unrealized-capital-gains.

cii Fordham, E. (2020). AOC: No one ever makes a billion dollars. You take a billion dollars. *Fox Business.* https://www.foxbusiness.com/money/aoc-billionaires-ta-nehisi-coates-interview

ciii Edwards, C. (2021). Democratic Tax Plan. *Cato Institute.* https://www.cato.org/blog/democratic-tax-plan

civ The National Constitution Center (2022). Common Interpretation: The Second Amendment. *Interactive Constitution.* https://constitutioncenter.org/interactive-constitution/interpretation/amendment-ii/interps/99

cv Tavernise, S. & Gebeloff, R. (2013). Share of homes with guns shows 4 decade decline. *The New York Times.* https://www.nytimes.com/2013/03/10/us/rate-of-gun-ownership-is-down-survey-shows.html

cvi Baichwal, R. (2022). Chicago shootings: 47 shot, 9 fatally over Memorial Day weekend, CPD says. *ABC 7 Chicago.* https://abc7chicago.com/chicago-shootings-shooting-memorial-day-weekend-violence/11911262/

cvii Lang, B. & Lang, M. (2021). Pandemics, protests, and firearms. *The American Journal of Health Economics, 7*(2). https://doi.org/10.1086/713035

cviii Kitroeff, N., Robles, F., Goodman, D. & Kovaleski, S. (2022). Police Response to Uvalde Shooting Infuriated Parents Clinging to Hope. *The New York Times.* https://www.nytimes.com/2022/05/26/us/uvalde-police-response-parents.html

[cix] Haworth, I. (2021). The Data Behind 'Mass Shootings,' And Why Democrat Proposals Aren't Likely To Help. *Daily Wire.* https://www.dailywire.com/news/the-data-behind-mass-shootings-and-why-democrat-proposals-arent-likely-to-help

[cx] Schaeffer, K. (2021). Key facts about Americans and guns. *Pew Research.* https://www.pewresearch.org/fact-tank/2021/09/13/key-facts-about-americans-and-guns/

[cxi] Ibid.

[cxii] Frontline (2013). *A social history of America's most popular drugs.* https://www.pbs.org/wgbh/pages/frontline/shows/drugs/buyers/socialhistory.html

[cxiii] Drugpolicy (2022). A history of the drug war. https://drugpolicy.org/issues/brief-history-drug-war

[cxiv] Ibid.

[cxv] Aguirre, L. (2021). Lessons learned and lost from a Vietnam-era study of addiction. *Stat.* https://www.statnews.com/2021/07/19/lessons-learned-and-lost-vietnam-era-addiction-study/

[cxvi] Vagins, D. & McCurdy, J. (2006). Cracks in the System: Twenty Years of the Unjust Federal Crack Cocaine Law. *American Civil Liberties Union.* https://www.aclu.org/other/cracks-system-20-years-unjust-federal-crack-cocaine-law

[cxvii] England, D. (2022). Crack vs. Powder Cocaine: One Drug, Two Penalties. *NOLO-Criminal Defense Lawyer.* https://www.criminaldefenselawyer.com/resources/crack-vrs-powder-cocaine-one-drug-two-penalties.htm

[cxviii] National Institute of Drug Abuse. (2022). *Opioid overdose crisis.* https://nida.nih.gov/drug-topics/opioids/opioid-overdose-crisis

[cxix] Taxel, S. (2022). Be Wary of Dubious Fentanyl Overdose Claims. *JEMS.* https://www.jems.com/patient-care/be-wary-of-dubious-fentanyl-overdose-claims/

[cxx] KFF (2020). *Opioid Overdose Deaths by Race/Ethnicity.* https://www.kff.org/other/state-indicator/opioid-overdose-deaths-by-

raceethnicity/?dataView=1&currentTimeframe=0&sortModel=%7B%2
2colId%22:%22Location%22,%22sort%22:%22asc%22%7D

cxxi Jaeger, K. (2022). Seven In Ten Biden Voters Support National
Marijuana Legalization, New Poll Finds. *Marijuana Moment.*
https://www.marijuanamoment.net/seven-in-ten-biden-voters-support-
national-marijuana-legalization-new-poll-finds/

cxxii Chung, A. (2022). Leaked draft abortion ruling a major blow to
Supreme Court, experts say. *Reuters.*
https://www.reuters.com/world/us/leaked-draft-abortion-ruling-major-
blow-supreme-court-experts-say-2022-05-03/

cxxiii Wikipedia (2022). Pre-Roe Precedents. *Abortion in the United States.*
https://en.wikipedia.org/wiki/Abortion_in_the_United_States#:~:text=
Prior%20to%20Roe%20v.,New%20York%20allowed%20abortions%
20generally.

cxxiv Kelly, M., et al. (2021). Activist Gloria Steinem reflects on abortion
rights as they hang in the balance. *NPR.*
https://www.npr.org/2021/12/09/1062791724/activist-gloria-steinem-
reflects-on-abortion-rights-as-they-hang-in-the-balance

cxxv Nawaz, A. & Buhre, M. (2022). Women reflect on what life was like
before Roe v. Wade. *PBS.*
https://www.pbs.org/newshour/show/women-reflect-on-what-life-was-
like-before-roe-v-wade

cxxvi Holland, J. (2016). Abolishing abortion: The history of the pro-life
movement in America. *Organization of American Historians.*
https://www.oah.org/tah/issues/2016/november/abolishing-abortion-
the-history-of-the-pro-life-movement-in-america/

cxxvii Ibid.

cxxviii Ibid.

cxxix North, A. (2019). How the abortion debate moved away from "safe,
legal, and rare." *Vox.* https://www.vox.com/2019/10/18/20917406/
abortion-safe-legal-and-rare-tulsi-gabbard

cxxx Yoder, K. (2015). #Shoutyourabortion makes front page of WaPo's Style
section. *mrcNewsBusters.*

https://www.newsbusters.org/blogs/culture/katie-yoder/2015/11/17/
shoutyourabortion-makes-front-page-wapos-style-section

cxxxi Hitchens, C. (2019). A left-wing atheist's case against abortion. *Crisis Magazine*. https://www.crisismagazine.com/2019/a-left-wing-atheists-case-against-abortion

cxxxii Shapiro, B. (2019). Democratic VA governor endorses murder of born-alive infants. *The Daily Wire*. https://www.dailywire.com/news/watch-democratic-va-governor-endorses-murder-born-ben-shapiro

cxxxiii Ibid.

cxxxiv Richardson, V. (2019). Most pro-choice adults oppose late-term abortion, denying newborns care: Poll. *AP News*. https://apnews.com/article/dec1f82c4c630cb97ab7cefc58cf0866

cxxxv Schowe, A. (2022). Illegal immigrant accused of raping, impregnating 10-year-old Ohio girl indicted by grand jury. *Daily Wire*. https://www.dailywire.com/news/illegal-immigrant-accused-of-raping-impregnating-10-year-old-ohio-girl-is-indicted-by-grand-jury

cxxxvi Reported legal abortions by race of women who obtained abortion by the state of occurrence (2019). *KFF*. https://www.kff.org/womens-health-policy/state-indicator/abortions-by-race/

cxxxvii Clegg, R. (2020). Percentage of births to unmarried women. *National Review*. https://www.nationalreview.com/corner/percentage-of-births-to-unmarried-women/

cxxxviii Center for Urban Renewal and Education (2015). The effects of abortion on the black community. *Congress.gov*. https://www.congress.gov/115/meeting/house/106562/witnesses/HHRG-115-JU10-Wstate-ParkerS-20171101-SD001.pdf

cxxxix Henderson, T. (2022). The Pandemic Prompted People to Move, But Many Didn't Go Far. *Pew*. https://www.pewtrusts.org/en/research-and-analysis/blogs/stateline/2022/03/23/the-pandemic-prompted-people-to-move-but-many-didnt-go-far

cxl Jones, J. (2018). In 14 states and DC, the African American unemployment rate is at least twice the white unemployment rate. *Economic Policy Institute*. https://www.epi.org/publication/state-race-unemployment-2018q1/

[cxli] David, G. (2022). NYC Black Unemployment Stuck Above 15%. *The City*. https://www.thecity.nyc/work/2022/2/15/22936440/nyc-black-unemployment-above-15-percent

[cxlii] Vargas, R. (2022). Getting back to work has been slower in California's Black community. *Spectrum News*. https://spectrumnews1.com/ca/la-west/business/2022/04/19/getting-back-to-work-california-black-community

[cxliii] Divounguy, O. (2022). Illinois' Black Workers Unemployed at Near Double U.S. Rate. *Illinois Policy*. https://www.illinoispolicy.org/illinois-black-workers-unemployed-at-near-double-u-s-rate/

[cxliv] US Census Bureau (2021). Census Bureau releases new data on minority-owned, veteran-owned, and women-owned businesses. *News Room*. https://www.census.gov/newsroom/press-releases/2021/characteristics-of-employer-businesses.html

[cxlv] Gitonga, S. (2022). How Many People Make Over 100k in a Year? *Spendmenot*. https://spendmenot.com/blog/how-many-people-make-over-100k

[cxlvi] Wahba, P. (2021). Only 19: The lack of Black CEOs in the history of the Fortune 500. *Fortune*. https://fortune.com/longform/fortune-500-black-ceos-business-history/

[cxlvii] Kingson, J. (2020). $1 billion-plus riot damage is most expensive in insurance history. *Axios*. https://www.axios.com/2020/09/16/riots-cost-property-damage

[cxlviii] Blitzer, R. (2021). Bail fund backed by Kamala Harris freed same rioter twice – now he's been charged again. *Fox News*. https://www.foxnews.com/politics/bail-fund-kamala-harris-thomas-moseley

[cxlix] Zaccardi, T. (2020). 'I've Had to Paint 'Black Owned Business' on My Minneapolis Bar During the Riots'. *Newsweek*. https://www.newsweek.com/paint-black-owned-business-bar-during-riots-1507398

[cl] Clayton, A. (2021). 'Walgreens fed my family': inside the San Francisco

stores closing over 'retail theft'. *The Guardian.*
https://www.theguardian.com/us-news/2021/nov/15/walgreens-
closures-san-francisco-crime-debate

cli Prestigiacomo, A. (2021). 14 Arrested In 'Smash-And-Grab' Thefts
Totaling $340,000, All Quickly Released Due To 'Zero Bail' Policy.
The Daily Wire. https://www.dailywire.com/news/14-arrested-in-smash-
and-grab-thefts-totaling-340000-all-quickly-released-due-to-zero-bail-
policy

clii Riley, J. (2021). The Predictable Consequences of 'Defund the Police'.
Wall Street Journal. https://www.wsj.com/articles/consequences-of-
defunding-the-police-libby-schaaf-violent-crime-rate-murder-public-
safety-11638915238

cliii Bidar, M. (2022). San Francisco votes overwhelmingly to recall
progressive DA Chesa Boudin. *CBS News.* https://www.cbsnews.com/
news/chesa-boudin-san-francisco-da-recalled/

cliv Ibid.

clv WIBC. (2019). AOC Mocks Flyover Country, Calls Electoral College A
'Racist Scam'. https://www.wibc.com/blogs/chicks/aoc-mocks-flyover-
country-calls-electoral-college-a-racist-scam/

clvi Food Research and Action Center (2022). *Rural Hunger.*
https://frac.org/hunger-poverty-america/rural-hunger

clvii Bentlage, D. (2022). The elephant in the room is destroying family
farms, rural communities and our democracy. *Missouri Independent.*
https://missouriindependent.com/2022/06/07/the-elephant-in-the-
room-is-destroying-family-farms-rural-communities-and-our-
democracy-opinion/

clviii Ibid.

clix Ibid.

clx Dress, B. (2022). Herbicide chemical linked to cancer found in majority
of urine samples in CDC study. *The Hill.*
https://thehill.com/policy/healthcare/3554147-herbicide-chemical-
linked-to-cancer-found-in-majority-of-urine-samples-in-cdc-study/

clxi Center for Food Safety (2005). *Monsanto vs U.S. Farmers.*

https://www.centerforfoodsafety.org/files/cfsmonsantovsfarmerreport11 305.pdf

clxii Mowrer, J. (2015). The Republican agriculture problem. *Des Moines Register*. https://www.desmoinesregister.com/story/opinion/columnists/2015/03/07/republicans-poor-agriculture-records/24550181/

clxiii National Alliance to End Homelessness (2021). *State of Homelessness: 2021 Edition*. https://endhomelessness.org/homelessness-in-america/homelessness-statistics/state-of-homelessness-2021/

clxiv Herman, T. (2018). Michael Knowles: Letting people live on the street is not showing compassion. *MyNorthwest*. https://mynorthwest.com/1140988/michael-knowles-letting-people-live-on-the-street-is-not-showing-compassion/

clxv Colton, E. (2022). Seattle businesses take law into own hands to combat homelessness, angering activists. *Fox News*. https://www.foxnews.com/us/seattle-businesses-take-law-hands-combat-homelessness-angering-activists

clxvi National Alliance to End Homelessness (2010). *What is a Continuum of Care?* https://endhomelessness.org/resource/what-is-a-continuum-of-care

clxvii Eide, S. (2020). Housing First and Homelessness: The Rhetoric and the Reality. *The Manhattan Institute*. https://www.manhattan-institute.org/housing-first-effectiveness

clxviii Rodgers, B. (2020). Utah was once lauded for solving homelessness — the reality was far more complicated. The *Salt Lake City Tribune*. https://www.sltrib.com/news/politics/2020/05/11/utah-was-once-lauded/

clxix Eide (2020).

CPSIA information can be obtained
at www.ICGtesting.com
Printed in the USA
LVHW091044221022
731319LV00004B/60